Theological Perspectives for Life, Liberty, and the Pursuit of Happiness

NEW APPROACHES TO RELIGION AND POWER

Series editor: Joerg Rieger

While the relationship of religion and power is a perennial topic, it only continues to grow in importance and scope in our increasingly globalized and diverse world. Religion, on a global scale, has openly joined power struggles, often in support of the powers that be. But at the same time, religion has made major contributions to resistance movements. In this context, current methods in the study of religion and theology have created a deeper awareness of the issue of power: Critical theory, cultural studies, postcolonial theory, subaltern studies, feminist theory, critical race theory, and working class studies are contributing to a new quality of study in the field. This series is a place for both studies of particular problems in the relation of religion and power as well as for more general interpretations of this relation. It undergirds the growing recognition that religion can no longer be studied without the study of power.

Series editor:
Joerg Rieger is Wendland-Cook Professor of Constructive Theology in the Perkins School of Theology at Southern Methodist University.

Titles:

No Longer the Same: Religious Others and the Liberation of Christian Theology
David R. Brockman

The Subject, Capitalism, and Religion: Horizons of Hope in Complex Societies
Jung Mo Sung

Imaging Religion in Film: The Politics of Nostalgia
M. Gail Hamner

Spaces of Modern Theology: Geography and Power in Schleiermacher's World
Steven R. Jungkeit

Transcending Greedy Money: Interreligious Solidarity for Just Relations
Ulrich Duchrow and Franz J. Hinkelammert

Foucault, Douglass, Fanon, and Scotus in Dialogue:
  On Social Construction and Freedom
Cynthia R. Nielsen

Lenin, Religion, and Theology
Roland Boer

In Search of God's Power in Broken Bodies: A Theology of Maum
Hwa-Young Chong

The Reemergence of Liberation Theologies: Models for the Twenty-First Century
Edited by Thia Cooper

Religion, Theology, and Class
Jeorg Rieger

Theological Perspectives for Life, Liberty, and the Pursuit of Happiness:
  Public Intellectuals for the Twenty-First Century
Edited by Ada María Isasi-Díaz, Mary McClintock Fulkerson, and
Rosemary P. Carbine

Theological Perspectives for Life, Liberty, and the Pursuit of Happiness

Public Intellectuals for the Twenty-First Century

Edited by
Ada María Isasi-Díaz,
Mary McClintock Fulkerson, and
Rosemary P. Carbine

First published in 2013 by
PALGRAVE MACMILLAN®
in the United States—a division of St. Martin's Press LLC,
175 Fifth Avenue, New York, NY 10010.

Where this book is distributed in the UK, Europe and the rest of the world,
this is by Palgrave Macmillan, a division of Macmillan Publishers Limited,
registered in England, company number 785998, of Houndmills,
Basingstoke, Hampshire RG21 6XS.

Palgrave Macmillan is the global academic imprint of the above companies
and has companies and representatives throughout the world.

Palgrave® and Macmillan® are registered trademarks in the United States,
the United Kingdom, Europe and other countries.

ISBN: 978–1–137–37170–6 (hardcover)
ISBN: 978–1–137–37222–2 (paperback)

Library of Congress Cataloging-in-Publication Data

Theological perspectives for life, liberty, and the pursuit of happiness :
public intellectuals for the twenty-first century / edited by Ada María
Isasi-Díaz, Mary McClintock Fulkerson, and Rosemary P. Carbine.
        pages cm
    Includes bibliographical references.
    ISBN 978–1–137–37170–6
        1. United States—Religion. 2. Religion and politics—United States.
    3. Religion and state—United States. 4. Life—Religious aspects.
    5. Liberty—Religious aspects. 6. Happiness—Religious aspects.
    I. Isasi-Díaz, Ada María, editor of compilation.

BL2525.T485 2013
320.97301—dc23   2013019294

A catalogue record of the book is available from the British Library.

Design by Newgen Knowledge Works (P) Ltd., Chennai, India.

First edition: November 2013

10 9 8 7 6 5 4 3 2 1

For Ada María
I Will Not Die an Unlived Life
Dawna Markova[1]
I will not die an unlived life.
I will not live in fear
of falling or catching fire.
I choose to inhabit my days,
to allow my living to open me,
to make me less afraid,
more accessible,
to loosen my heart
until it becomes a wing,
a torch, a promise.
I choose to risk my significance;
to live so that which came to me as seed
goes to the next as blossom
and that which came to me as blossom,
goes on as fruit.

---

[1] In Dawna Markova, *I Will Not Die An Unlived Life: Reclaiming Purpose and Passion* (Berkeley, CA: Conari Press, 2000). Used with permission.

Contents

Foreword

Joerg Rieger

Power is all-pervasive in our lives; it is at work not only in politics and economics but also the in worlds of culture and ideas, and in matters of religion. At the same time, power is never unilinear. It takes many different shapes and forms. Dominant forms of power often move from the top down and seek to control everything. The good news, however, presented in this book, is that there are other forms of power that move from the bottom up and provide alternatives that are often overlooked as the dominant powers seek to deny their existence and to cover them up. One of the most important developments in religion and theology is a sense that these fields can no longer be studied without paying attention to these flows of power.

In this book, the authors analyze the stark shapes that dominant power takes in our age, but they do so with the goal to identify alternative forms of power that direct us toward new visions and new ways of life. These alternative forms of power emerge in various places and among various groups of people and they are not easily harmonized, but they share in common the fact that they emerge from the grassroots, from locations that are frequently neglected by those who present themselves as the gatekeepers of common sense, intellectuals and academics included.

It is no accident that this book owes its existence to the initiative of Ada María Isasi-Díaz. She was the one who convinced a group of intellectuals involved in public issues to produce short chapters that address not only the most burning issues of our time but also the hope that emerges here and the alternatives that are being birthed. This initiative was deeply rooted in the heart of her work and in how she thought of herself and of her friends as public intellectuals.

As a result, the chapters of this book are down-to-earth and written to make a difference in the midst of the struggles of contemporary life. At the same time, these efforts represent a cataclysmic change in our fields of study, of which Ada María was one of the pioneers. While many of us were still trained to study religion and theology in terms of the seemingly universal ideas of the elites, we are now increasingly paying attention to everyday expressions of life. In her native Spanish idiom, Ada María kept talking about "lo cotidiano," the everyday, as that which is at the heart of the study of religion and theology.

It is the life experience of the common people, and the marginalized in particular, that forces us to pay attention to the structures of power; the elites, on the other hand, can afford to take power for granted. And it is in these life experiences of the common people that we find the alternatives. The common people, as Ada María knew so well, are not simply the victims of dominant power but are those who put up resistance and who present us with alternatives that provide real hope. These everyday struggles, as the dangerous memories of some of the Christian and other religious traditions attest, are also the location of the divine.

Another key insight that marks the sea change in which we find ourselves is the awareness of struggle. This is another one of Ada María's contributions: we do not find ourselves in a situation of heavenly bliss where people for the most part get along—we find ourselves in the midst of struggles that are matters of life and death. Ada María learned this from her sisters at the grassroots—Latina women who are forced to struggle for survival and against the forces of death every day. How far US society and the academy are removed from understanding this can be seen in the fact that those who take stands against exploitation and oppression are often accused of instigating class struggle. Ada María was one of the intellectuals who helped us understand that the struggle doesn't come from only one place or form of power; rather, the struggle that is waged here is initiated from the bottom up and from the top down. In this context, the goal of our everyday struggles against exploitation and oppression is not the struggle itself but a new life, which overcomes struggle and the daily grind.

The sea change of which Ada María's work and the present book are a part challenges not just traditional academic methods but also the American way of life. Rather than starting with lofty ideals and grand dreams—the so-called power of positive thinking—we are now starting from the everyday struggles of life and the hopes that are located here. From there we are building the vision that does not rest until it ushers into the "kin-dom" of God—a term that summarizes of Ada María's theological efforts to reenvision the difference that the divine makes in the world in non-imperial terms. What more could we ask for?

Introduction: Reimagining the Responsibilities of Public Intellectuals

Ada María Isasi-Díaz, Mary McClintock Fulkerson, and Rosemary P. Carbine

What binds this nation together is not the colors of our skin or the tenets of our faith or the origins of our names. What makes us exceptional—what makes us American—is our allegiance to an idea, articulated in a declaration made more than two centuries ago: "We hold these truths to be self-evident, that all men are created equal, that they are endowed by their Creator with certain unalienable rights, that among these are Life, Liberty, and the pursuit of Happiness." Today we continue a never-ending journey, to bridge the meaning of those words with the realities of our time. For history tells us that while these truths may be self-evident, they have never been self-executing.... That is our generation's task—to make these words, these rights, these values—of Life, and Liberty, and the Pursuit of Happiness—real for every American.... You and I, as citizens, have the obligation to shape the debates of our time— not only with the votes we cast, but with the voices we lift in defense of our most ancient values and enduring ideals.

With these words, President Barack Hussein Obama in his second inaugural address on January 21, 2013 enjoined all US citizens to do the collective work of public intellectuals as their political birthright. Yet, "public intellectual" is a term and a role often rife with misconceptions, and some of the contributors to this book rightly express reservations about using it. *Public* can be misconstrued to mean those who have garnered both academic affluence and broad societal influence. *Intellectual* can also falsely imply a privileged academic scholar at an institution of higher education, suspected of participating in status quo power relations and thus perceived to be distanced from the vicissitudes of daily life. Rather than academic rock stars or celebrities who have cornered (and benefitted from!) the market on doing serious thinking about important public issues with a social impact, "public intellectual" in this book refers to scholar-activists or activist-thinkers who work with various communities of accountability in and beyond the academy (e.g. feminist movements, racial and/or economic justice activism, pacifist groups), who question the prevalent ideological contours and values that shape and structure our public or common life, and who engage in critical thought as well as sociopolitical action for justice—all of which flow from a shared sense of being human with others and seeking flourishing for all.

The assertion that as academics we have the moral responsibility to be public intellectuals is thus not a self-aggrandizing claim, but rather an embrace of the responsibility we have to enhance the society we have inherited, in which we live, and to which we contribute. Our understanding of this responsibility and our desire to write about it arises in response to the absolute need we have to live life intentionally, to seriously analyze the influence we have with those who study with us, and, given the great investment society has made in us, the absolute right society has to demand that we contribute to its upbuilding. Embracing our moral responsibility to contribute to society is an important way of repaying a social investment, such as the money society has spent on us in the form of scholarships and grants, and the time that society has given us to pursue our own interests, which we always hope reverberates for the good of all. While many of the contributors express gratitude for inspiring teachers, financial and collegial support, and the communities of inquiry offered by the academy, many of us also recognize the importance of transformative pedagogy, to help not only ourselves but also our students unlearn harmful patterns of race, class, gender, sexual, and other forms of privilege that are life-denying, distort liberty, and obstruct happiness. The responsibility we have to be public intellectuals needs to be much more broadly embraced in the contemporary United States, but at the same time this role needs to be further clarified.

We must have an impact on our sociohistorical reality because, as academics, we have the opportunity to influence the worldview that guides us as a nation, as a society, and as a people. At present, there is much talk about the need for creating a "new" America. Given the failures of economic and political systems during the past few years, this most important and absolute need must not be the work of a few but rather must emerge from the people. Our government must follow the people's understandings of the values that must guide us. All those who hold governmental positions at all levels must remember everyday that in the United States, very explicitly, government is "of the people, by the people, for the people," as Abraham Lincoln so magnificently instructed us in his Gettysburg Address.

Activists have led the way in this struggle to reconceptualize what the United States should represent and advocate as a people and as a nation. Reviewing some significant events of recent years, we have to be grateful to those who struggled mightily against the governor of Wisconsin to protect union rights. These activists brought home the Arab Spring—the spontaneous protests of common people that started across the Arab world in early 2011 and is still going on in Syria—making us realize that we too could bring about radical change in our government and in our society. Wisconsin activists also parented the Occupy Wall Street Movement that has propagated like wildfire from New York to other US cities as well as to more than 80 cities throughout the world.

Those who oppose the Occupy Movement criticize it for not making concrete demands, for not having clear plans for the future. Those of us who support the Occupy Movement know that before concrete demands are made, values need to be identified, and a vision rooted in the needs and hopes of the people must be articulated. The questions that are raised by the activists—and by many of us whom the dominant status quo political and economic systems have failed miserably—provide the needed guidelines for elaborating a new United States, one that holds those with economic resources, prestige, and power, accountable, one that rescues politics and government from the hands of corporate America and returns it to the people, and one that creates a moral economy in which basic human needs trump profit.

Academics have a vital role to play in creating and explaining a new national identity that entails and inspires these humanitarian values. Our many years of study must free us to serve the new vision emerging from the people, rather than support present-day structures that have failed miserably. Our mission as public intellectuals does not demand taking the side of any given political or social system. Rather, our mission is to impact the shape of society—of social, economic, and political institutions—by clarifying the goals behind the political and economic priorities of those who govern. Our role as academics embracing our responsibility to be public intellectuals begins by acknowledging our worldview. Lincoln's phrase becomes so very valuable here, because what must guide us, the vision that beckons us, is indeed the people, the people as a whole and never the few who are always privileged at the expense of the many, and particularly those whom present-day systems have failed. Modeling the meaning of representing issues of justice to the wider public, Ada María, who first imagined this project, exemplified and continues to inspire this vocation for academics. Ada understood herself to be a public intellectual, or, as she put it, an activist-theologian, whose experience was deeply rooted in enduring and effective struggles for justice for the marginalized. She came to the United States with her family in 1960 as a political refugee from Cuba. As an Ursuline sister, she spent years in Lima, Peru working with the poor. After leaving the order in 1969, Ada's conversion to feminism in the 1970's and experiences with the Women's Ordination Conference were also crucial to her formation. As she continued to be connected to grassroots Latinas whom she regarded as organic intellectuals, all of these experiences helped her see the intersection of a number of marginalizing factors besides gender and the potentially liberative role of Christianity, and religion more generally, in ongoing struggles for life. These experiences were and remained rich sources for Ada María's life as an ethicist at Drew University, an academic who never confined herself to the so-called ivory tower. Instead, she worked to create "a praxis of solidarity with other communities of struggle. . . . convinced that unless we build common understandings and practices among those of us who are marginalized, our communities will continue to be denied access to what they need for fullness of life" (Isasi-Díaz 2004, 5–6).

Based on the paradigmatic character of Ada María's life as a public intellectual, our field of action is the culture of the United States—the American way of life that has been absconded by the few and set against the many both in this country and the world over. By rethinking the values that must undergird us as a people, as a society, as a nation, and that must be the immediate basis for all government, we can stake the claim that the American way of life must be based on "life, liberty and the pursuit of happiness," as the Declaration of Independence sets forth, not on greed, crass individualism, and egotism. As public intellectuals, we must explore and reclarify the meaning of life, liberty, and happiness in order to effectively combat economic profit, controlling and dominating power, and dishonorable prestige, in order to uproot them from our hearts, lives, and social structures. To do so, we must unmask historical and present-day structures that have not and do not yet fully realize these values, as well as strive to elucidate and establish the true meaning of life for all, of liberty grounded in solidarity, and of happiness as the fulfillment of human capabilities, rather than a consumerist fed and bred acquisition of anything and everything we can own.

As public intellectuals, one of our most valuable tools for this task is words. Our words have to be measured and must be addressed first of all to ourselves. We must pledge never to use words "cleverly" for they can indeed become a tool for propaganda that might move people but leave them empty and diminished as human beings. We must never appeal to prejudices, emotions, vanities, and expectations of the people to incense them and turn them into a mob that stops thinking about the consequences of their actions and stops being rational. Our words must always illumine, never hide the truth. Our words must appeal to reason and help people to respond from their best self, which is always a social self that recognizes and practices compassion, not a self-centered individual who has made herself or himself exclusively into a *homo economicus*. We must never simply throw words at people but must seek to engage them in reasonable arguments out of which can grow shared understandings about the good of all. In order to do so, our words must never be violent but they must be aggressive, confronting irrationality in such a way that words become community-building tools, not divisive and hate-fomenting.

In our role as public intellectuals, always from the perspective of the people, for the people, and by the people, our task revolves around and is always focused on systemic change, on structural change. Of course, persons are indeed most important, but our task is to move our society and to move us as a people, so that we can create radical change in our form of government—from a representative democracy that stops representing only the corporate world and the wealthy and again represents all the people; in our economy—from profit-centered to human needs–centered; and, in our society—from privileging the few to providing for the development of the capabilities of the many.

As public intellectuals, our goal parallels the goal of all education: developing a critical consciousness. Developing critical consciousness entails a social and psychological process. As a process, it is a dynamic movement similar to the Occupy Wall Street Movement that started in the summer of 2011 in New York City. Those who oppose the Occupy Movement criticize its lack of definition. But processes have less to do with being and more to do with becoming. Critical consciousness is precisely a process of becoming that hopefully will last our entire lives. As a psychological process, developing critical consciousness is a coming to know ourselves, made possible by acting and reflecting on our actions. Furthermore, this critical self-knowledge is not, and cannot be, an individual act. Because human beings are social beings, our interconnectedness shapes how we come to know ourselves and how we come to be ourselves. Very seldom can we uphold who we are, act out of who we are, and act in order to become ourselves if we do not have societal structures that facilitate such movements. The Occupy Movement and other ways of organizing open up spaces for us to continually develop a critical consciousness. Developing critical consciousness "implies socialization and the transmission of culture, not in an adaptive sense, but rather in a creative and revolutionary way" (Martín-Baró 1991, 226).

Ada María's experience as an immigrant to the United States and her continued identification with marginalized groups gave her a crucial consciousness that has been vital to challenging the status quo in North American culture. Her invention and elaboration of *mujerista* theology has served as a profoundly important way to give voice to often over-looked Hispana/Latina women (Isasi-Díaz 2004 [1993]). By focusing on and writing out of the quotidian or everyday experiences and wisdom of Latinas, Ada María has challenged not only the false universalizing of academic feminist thinking about women's experience; she has also creatively complexified issues of racism and ethnic marginalization beyond the Black-white binary by redefining diversity and pluralism in light of Latina and Latino experiences. She combined *mestizaje* (the mixture of white and Native peoples living in what is now Latin America and the Caribbean) with *mulatez* (the mixture of Black and white peoples) to recover and make visible the racial and cultural mixtures of Spanish, Amerindian, and African peoples embodied by US Latinas and Latinos. Ada María acknowledged both the violent colonialist legacies of this intermixture and the new forms of *mestizaje* and *mulatez* happening in the United States, both to describe our reality of intermingled peoples and cultures and to make it a moral choice (Isasi-Díaz 1996, 64–66, 79–80). Her life and writings thus stand as a creative and revolutionary model for continued academic connection and identification with marginalized groups and unheard voices.

As academic theologians and religion scholars inspired by Ada María's work, our task resonates with other academics who understand themselves as public intellectuals. While we ground our words in human values, we come to those human values from a religious perspective. Religion does not add content to human values but rather "thematizes" those human values (Curran 1985, 11), making them concrete and explicit in the language and texts, symbols, and practices associated with religious traditions that revere Jesus Christ, the Buddha, the prophet Muhammad, the Jewish Torah, and the Hindu Vedas. Although most of the contributors to this book identify as Christian theologians or ethicists, we do not wield religion as a weapon or use it as a ruse in irrational appeals. Instead, we are compelled by the belief in the sanctity of life and in the human values that arise out of a social ontology, or our interconnectedness with each other as well as with other species and the biosphere.

This call to be public intellectuals invites us to make new myths for America, which tie its guiding principles of life, liberty, and the pursuit of happiness not to what Cornel West calls the "three dominating, antidemocratic dogmas" of free-market fundamentalism, militarism, and authoritarianism (West 2004, 3–8), but to new and more prophetic meanings. As William Dean notes, "If the religious critic's responsibility [as a public intellectual] is to be exercised, new thought must be given to the myth of America" (Dean 1994, 174). To be viable, a new myth will emerge from "the deliberate development of conventions about American meanings, including religious meanings. . . . It will frame a sense of the whole from a particular public standpoint. It will offer large visions that provide images in terms of which all else in the society can be understood." (Dean 1994, 176) Resonating with and building on this rich tradition of scholars who understand themselves as public intellectuals, that is, intellectuals who serve the public good and, like West, who seek to give prophetic witness that "speaks to the democratic issues of equality of opportunity, service to the poor, and a focus on the public interest" (West 2004, 17–19, 74), these essays are most deeply inspired by Ada María's passion for the constant need to challenge long-standing traditions, whether Christian or secular, through the lens of *la lucha* or the struggle for justice. Thus, these essays result from a creative bricolage of religious, cultural, and so-called national values, which aims to reimagine and revivify US common life, to construct new practices and strategies for altering our current sociopolitical imagination and way of life. These essays certainly do not claim to address or resolve all contemporary social and political dilemmas in the United States, or conclude with one shared set of strategies to reimagine a shared American mythos and ethos. Nonetheless, the call for academics to be public intellectuals and Ada María's model as an activist-theologian remind us that our social location needs to give us a real connection to marginalized groups. Similar to The Poverty Tour: A Call to Conscience, an event during which Cornel West and Tavis Smiley visited 18 cities in 11 states during August 2011 to listen to the stories of everyday poor peoples' plights, or the organic connection of Ada María who lived with the poor and never separated herself from *lo cotidiano* or the everyday lives of marginalized groups, the contributors to this collection have a shared stake in what happens in America, not simply the freedom to do a kind of academic tourism of so-called outsiders.

The logic of these essays is inspired by some of Ada María's characteristic convictions: the crucial role of learning from the experiences of others, especially disempowered groups, involved in *la lucha* or the struggle for justice; the centrality of *lo cotidiano* or the everyday for innovative epistemologies and ethics, or ways of knowing and living; and, the testimony of her life to the significance of *fuerzas para la lucha* or God-given strength for the struggle. Beginning in Part I with the view from the struggles of marginalized groups about our understanding of the public that is America, Part II moves to examples of everyday practices that emerge from complex social contexts and realities and that urge us to reconfigure our general categories of ethics, theology, and politics. Part 3 engages with the function of religion and of a God-referent in the work for justice, concluding with the challenge to both religion and humanism in contemporary US politics.

To actually help in shaping a society that works for the good of all is no easy task, as these essays illustrate. As Part I illustrates, our official national founding story misrepresents realities of power; in particular, our story attests to the denial by the Euro-invaders who supposedly discovered America of their own status as invasive immigrants. Historically in the United States, religion, and particularly Christian faith, has authorized the colonizing of Native land, generated a religious reasoning that justified slavery or the continued avoidance of racialized realities, or produced authoritarian and theocratic nationalist views that trade on, and indeed valorize, individualism that currently buttresses status quo inequalities, political or economic. These grim reminders that religious, and often Christian, visions and values do not necessarily support our commitment to a shared common good, especially one that privileges the most marginalized, do not rule out its constructive and liberative work, especially when rethought and reconfigured through the strikingly creative visions of "life, liberty and the pursuit of happiness" provided in this book. In response to religion's ability to both oppress and liberate, to both dehumanize and enhance human well-being, these essays all practice what Linell Cady has called extensional theology in order to claim a public voice and role, "to extend fairly the existing political order and to improve that order." This method involves retrieving, rethinking, and extending aspects of religious, cultural, and political symbols, texts, and practices in new ways to better address contemporary sociopolitical situations (Cady 1993, 56, 57, 62–64).

Based on Ada María's emphasis on *la vida es la lucha* or struggle as partly constitutive of life, Part I draws on the wisdom from different social and historical struggles to redefine "our nation" and its values. Andrea Smith rereads "our nation" from a viewpoint that has been honed by her many years as an activist in antiviolence and indigenous peoples movements. With a deeply profound personal as well as intellectual awareness of our nation's egregious history, she starts with a forthright condemnation of the double standard of the United States in denouncing genocide as a violation of civil rights and democracy happening elsewhere while ignoring that US law sanctioned the genocide of Native Americans and the violation of their civil rights and right to self-determination. Smith challenges us to rethink our present understanding of nationalism and sovereignty, which, she suggests, "inevitably lead to xenophobia, intolerance, factionalism, and violence. All sovereignty or nationalist struggles, it seems, are headed down that slippery slope towards the ethnic cleansing witnessed in Bosnia." The author boldly invites the reader not to presume that the United States "should or will always continue to exist as a nation-state"; to do so creates the space needed "to reflect on what exactly is a just form of governance, not only for Native peoples, but for the rest of the world." She focuses on the spiritually-based visions of nation and sovereignty, separate from nation-states, which Native women activists are beginning to articulate, which "are predicated on interrelatedness and responsibility." Following a critique of heteropatriarchy and the current understanding of human relationship to land, Smith concludes her article by endorsing "mass-based peoples' movements" that use "alternative governmental structures," instead of relying on the state. These movements make military power obsolete and depend on principles of horizontalism that make possible "radical participatory rather than representational democracy." The author grounds her proposal on actual happenings taking place among factory workers in Argentina and self-governing Native communities in places like Chiapas, Mexico.

James Evans, an intellectual who has always seen and experienced the connection of texts and lived realities, provides a compelling reread of "our nation's" history as he illustrates the very different constraints on access to life, liberty, and the pursuit of happiness that have always accompanied race. Political power, economics, and morality are all intertwined with race and religion. Even as African American religious visions have offered life-giving interpretations of liberty for racialized populations, our systems have found ways to render inequality as "normal." Whether by racist policies that limited the social contract to whites, or by contemporary versions of "you deserve what you've got," the function of our national systems has continued to reproduce both political and economic inequality. Showing how intertwined the US moral and religious imagination has long been with race, Evans, a theologian trained in literature, political science, and ministry, reminds us that the function of religion based upon Jeffersonian and Hobbesian reason basically supported the view that the powerful were those who rightly ruled. Even as happiness is part of a moral narrative, he argues, the limitations of white versions of that imagination were disturbingly illustrated by the dominant interpretation of the Black Power Movement as a threat rather than the creative use of American values in a crucial movement for justice.

Sharon Welch asks who we are as Americans and what our role in the world is today, based on a reinterpretation of "our nation's" thinking about strength and power. Welch discusses two main visions: one, believed by many, that genuine power and decisive action require unilateral military force; another, that coercive military force can be counterproductive. This latter one is not merely about the "folly of military intervention in particular situations... but another vision of world community and of the ways peoples and governments can exercise power responsibly in the face of grave threats and great opportunities." With years of activist experience in peacebuilding and racial justice, Welch endorses a different definition of strength and power from the operative one today. For her, such a definition must include seeing the world through the eyes of others beyond the shores of the United States, including the different religious traditions that have been mainly ignored or maligned in our history. With a vision that is especially enriched through her significant work enabling academic institutional change, Welch ends with a clarion call to endorse peace, "viable alternatives" to reverence, compassion, virtuosity, honesty, curiosity, and respect, which she proposes as "wagers to be lived, risks to be taken, not conundrums to be resolved in theory."

In keeping with Ada María's persistent point about *lo cotidiano* or the everyday as the locus of theology, ethics, and politics, Part II focuses on emancipatory and life-giving practices that emerge from particular contexts and struggles. Inspired in part by her work with a nonprofit organization for ex-Korean military wives, K. Christine Pae defines excessive militarization as a global reality. An academic who regularly works with ordinary believers as well as her students around social justice issues, Pae explores in this essay how Americans, as global citizens, can rediscover the sacrality of all human life, responsibly exercise political liberty, and pursue happiness with others. To do this, Pae explores everyday practices, especially narrative and storytelling, of women and men whose lives are threatened by globalized American militarism, especially South Korean sex workers in US military camptowns, and as a result of those narratives rearticulates global peacebuilding and spiritual activism grounded in ordinary people's everyday lives.

A wonderfully creative interpretation of pleasure and joy in our pursuit of happiness is found in Paula Cooey's exploration of the previously unacknowledged constructive functions of daily religious practices of self-denial in ascetic (i.e. vowed religious) communities. Another scholar with wisdom shaped by years of activism in the public sphere, in churches, and publishing on social justice issues around gender, race, environmentalism and class issues relative to religion, Cooey reinterprets some classic stereotypes. Reminding us that asceticism is really about training, crucial to any successful pursuit of happiness—including the shaping of desire—Cooey connects the practices of sixteenth-century Anabaptists and a Roman Catholic sisters' community with the production of freedom and happiness. Rather than the repression of desire, world rejection, and moralistic self-denigration stereotypically associated with asceticism, the asceticism of these communities profoundly enhances the values of the American Dream. Anabaptists, for example, have lived out and supported religious freedom in their own distinctive way. Ascetic practices of the Sisters of St. Joseph of Carondelet have enhanced the options for person-centered medical care by working with other denominations. Ongoing attitudes of joy and hope are based neither on success nor belief in an afterlife, but seem to confirm that self-denial as engagement for the "other" can provide a happiness that is basic and sustaining, rather than diminishing and repressive.

Teresa Delgado recalls the alternative liberative rereadings of Christian Gospels by African Americans while confronting the realities of the transatlantic slave trade that left many deceased Africans under water en route to the Americas. A creative thinker with an ongoing commitment to the intersection of belief in social justice and its practice, including activism in coalition work for peace, Delgado explores and enhances these rereadings that radically rearticulated the slave-holding and patriarchal US founding fathers' version of "life, liberty and happiness." Based on this exploration of everyday resistance to racism, both historical and contemporary, Delgado aptly describes the new slavery and its racially marked economic realities of being under water from un/underemployment as one way to prompt re-reading of those Gospels for more liberative meanings. In contrast to Wall Street creeds and prosperity gospels that equate life and happiness with individual material wealth and well-being, Delgado leverages baptism in a religious, sociopolitical, and economic sense of new life and gives a profound reinterpretation of Gospel resources on happiness, the Beatitudes, in a way that gives voice to new practices that may yet yield new life.

The "logic of downturn" or the collapse of middle-class visions of the American Dream (job security, economic stability, and a social safety net) brought on by the nightmare of the Great Recession since 2007 inspires Joerg Rieger to seek out other horizons for the flourishing of life that is collective, is focused on the people, and prioritizes the ability of all to live well. From this perspective and experience in community organizing, Rieger redefines solidarity as an on-the-ground living of these values in order to meet everyday needs and to agitate for social change. With knowledge based upon long-term work with labor movements, Rieger calls for more radical solidarity to replace both current congregational and corporate-sponsored charity and volunteer work. For Rieger, deep solidarity is founded on a shared stake in our common life, is oriented toward forging a common bond in times of economic crises, and celebrates shared labor of creating and recreating society, beginning at the grassroots.

Mark Lewis Taylor pushes for further recognition of the intersections between the theological and the political through aesthetic or artful practices of human creativity. With an imagination shaped by years of antiwar activism and very focused work for prison reform, Taylor insists that a rethinking of "theological" and "political" is not a new solely academic enterprise. Rather, he argues, this rethinking offers further support and respect for the non-dualistic ways that the power of exploited and excluded groups is displayed in such art-forces as painting, dancing, singing, marching, walking, and quilting. An activist with a passion for the importance of critical reflection, his reimagining from on-the-ground liberative energies invites a compelling alternative understanding of life and liberty as liberation, based on a retelling of Jesus's ministerial practices and way of the cross found in contemporary novels.

Part III interrogates both the possibilities and the limits of Ada María's argument for God-given strength in struggles for a more emancipatory and flourishing life. Offering a vital contribution to the development of critical consciousness, Anthony Pinn observes that for too long the public discourse of Christian faith and its vision of our common life "has not safeguarded the welfare of the collective community in all its diversity," insisting that we must now learn to do that. Arguing that theistic religion too often functions as a form of world-denial, directing believers *away* from the physicality of the world, Pinn proposes a materialist biological grounding for shared humanity in order to galvanize our commitment to the common good. For the vision of collective life to include the full spectrum of human pleasure, we must focus on our crucial biological desires and the common ethical commitments our mutual biological needs demand. Pinn's negative take on the function of theistic religion offers a crucial corrective for the theological imagination, and, importantly, it does not end in a mandate for atheism. Rather, his criticism entails a generous call for crucial conversations between moderates of all sides in order to extend the meaning of "life, liberty and happiness" to deeper support for human accountability, pleasure, and well-being. That generosity is wonderfully displayed in his long-term activism with a wide variety of humanitarian institutions, from African American and American Humanist, to Unitarian Universalist, among others.

A critical take on the function of belief in God is Mary McClintock Fulkerson's attempt at a potentially liberative reading of the national mantra of "one nation under God." Offering a rereading of this theocentric American value, Fulkerson argues that the God-related grounding of life, liberty, and the pursuit of happiness should not be interpreted as a requirement for either a Christian nation or any religious belief. At least for believers who are not likely to give up their religious faith, this mantra should rather be interpreted as the iconoclasm or self-criticism inherent in theocentric faith, namely, the refusal to absolutize any worldly finite identity or reality, social or otherwise. A posture for the enhancement of world-engagement, rather than denial or avoidance of world, materiality and all its pleasures, iconoclasm entails self-criticism linked to the addressing of injustice and power imbalances. Self-criticism by the powerful in relation to the plight of marginalized populations will begin to generate rewritten accounts of American history that have occluded the marginalized. Shaped by her work with a local public project to recover Durham, North Carolina's social history of racism, sexism, and other injustices, Fulkerson recognizes that deeply internalized aversions to the "other" are at the root of the injustice of American practices. Addressing injustice has not been fixed by rationality or legislation, or by ostensibly "inclusive" churches populated by dominant populations. Minimally, such change requires alternative face-to-face communities of accountability that will alter our dominant stereotypes of one another.

Stephanie Mitchem's essay focuses on how the political divide we experience in the United States today is profoundly religious: on the one hand, religious conservatives work to construct the United States into the Christian nation as they alone define it; on the other hand, "activists work to create greater equity around the world, informed by ethical and religious values that they work to infuse into political values." Having long recognized "the cognitive dissonances between lived life and theoretical pronouncements" of mainline (white) disciplines, Mitchem's intellectual activism is shaped by years of "asking questions" as an African American, middle-class woman about the false universalizing of white American/European experience. Mitchem complicates her work further as she opens to view key social justice issues entailed in contemporary faith divides—issues that rarely get public exposure. Focusing in particular on the functions of religious conservatism in national political debates, Mitchem shows that this vision brings "profound confusion about the ends of society and the meaning of community," denying the obligation to help the poor, to reduce or do away with so-called entitlement projects that provide a social safety net for the most vulnerable, opposing unions and just pay for teachers, and so forth. This vision relies on a "hate speech" that is "so sophisticated that the number of disenfranchised, numb, apathetic people increases." Though not always using religious language, the activists endorse "power *with*" rather than "power *over*," an understanding of freedom that cannot be separated from the struggle for human dignity and non-hierarchical organization as well as leadership. These understandings are indeed religious for many and need to be claimed as such.

Aligning with Cornel West's diagnosis of nihilism in America, an increasing stratification, polarization, and fragmentation in US civil society motivates Rosemary Carbine to critically examine recent events in US conservative and liberal political camps in order to explore their alternative political visions of reviving the common good, often rooted in what Americans revere as civil religion. Based on an analysis of the operative civil religion in Glenn Beck's Restoring Honor rally in 2010 and in the PBS-sponsored By The People citizen deliberations during and beyond 2007, Carbine offers a compelling model of dialogue rooted in humanistic virtues of listening, learning, respect, and compassion for the renewing of civil society. For Carbine, life in a democracy is partly oriented to public discourse and decision making through that discourse; gaining recognition and participating in that discourse via the practice of these virtues is part of enjoying and sustaining a shared life together in a democracy that esteems dialogue—and much more.

Influenced by her activism in US Catholic feminist movements and her scholarly work in comparative feminist, womanist, and *mujerista* theologies as well as US public/political theologies, Carbine considers the classroom a site of civil society; she utilizes transformative pedagogies to help shape undergraduate students for informed, responsible, and justice-oriented citizenship.

The book concludes with Ada María Isasi-Díaz's essay about the too often ignored constructive contributions of immigrant groups to the United States. in redefining life, liberty, and the pursuit of happiness, particularly from the perspectives of Latinas and Latinos. After highlighting some of the very little known (or perhaps purposefully ignored) history of one of Latinas/Latinos ancestors—the Spanish—in what was US territory even before the arrival of the Pilgrims, Isasi-Díaz discusses facts about present-day immigration that are hardly ever considered, such as immigration as an intrinsic element of globalization and the responsibility of the United States for creating conditions in other countries that consequently coerce peoples to migrate in order to survive. Isasi-Díaz claims the right of immigrants to contribute to redefining who US citizens are and what the United States is about. She argues for the need for a broader "we" when it comes to understanding who constitutes the people of the United States as a nation. She ends by explicitly mentioning Latinas'/Latinos' contributions to this nation: an understanding of life as a struggle, the importance of relationships captured in their valuing of family that is not merely a heteropatriarchal one but celebrated in Latinas'/Latinos' *fiestas*, and the importance of community over individualism and destructive competitiveness. Isasi-Díaz believes that these Latina/Latino cultural values are indeed most valuable in creating a postnational project of humanization of which the United States must be a part.

We, the scholars whose works appear in this book are grateful to be able to exercise our role as public intellectuals and to contribute at this time of crisis—a time of radical possibilities as well as of enormous difficulties—to the creation of a new United States of America committed to the life of all peoples and species spending ourselves to provide for the full development of all of our capabilities as an exercise of liberty, and rejoicing in the happiness that true solidarity can bring as we are and we in the US slowly become a people for the good of all.

References

Cady, Linell. 1993. *Religion, Theology, and American Public Life*. Albany: State University of New York Press.

Curran, Charles. 1985. *Directions in Fundamental Moral Theology*. Notre Dame: University of Notre Dame Press.

Dean, William. 1994. *The Religious Critic in American Culture*. Albany: State University of New York Press.

Ellacuría, Ignacio. 1991. "Is a Different Kind of University Possible?" In *Towards a Society that Serves Its People—The Intellectual Contribution of El Salvador's Murdered Jesuits,* edited by John Hassett and Hugh Lacey. Washington, DC: Georgetown University Press.

Isasi-Díaz, Ada María. 1996. *Mujerista Theology: A Theology for the Twenty-First Century*. Maryknoll, NY: Orbis Books.

———. 2004. *La Lucha Continues: Mujerista Theology*. Maryknoll, NY: Orbis Books.

———. 2004 [1993]. *En La Lucha/In the Struggle: Elaborating a Mujerista Theology*. 10th anniversary edition. Minneapolis: Fortress Press.

Martín-Baró, Ignacio. 1991. "Developing a Critical-Consciousness through the University Curriculum." In *Towards a Society that Serves Its People—The Intellectual Contribution of El Salvador's Murdered Jesuits*, edited by John Hassett and Hugh Lacey. Washington, DC: Georgetown University Press.

The Poverty Tour: A Call to Conscience. 2011. On five episodes of the PBS *Tavis Smiley Show*. Available at http://www.pbs.org/wnet/tavissmiley/features/poverty-tour/.

West, Cornel. 2004. *Democracy Matters*. New York: Penguin Books.

PART I

Learning about "Our Nation" from
La Lucha *(The Struggle)*

CHAPTER 1

The Indigenous Dream—A World without an "America"

Andrea Smith

Post 9/11, even radical scholars such as Judith Butler and Amy Kaplan framed George Bush's policies as an attack on the US Constitution. For instance, Butler described Bush's policies as a "suspension of law" (Butler 2004, 55) whereby the nation can, in the name of "sovereignty," act against "existing legal frameworks, civil, military, and international... Under this mantle of sovereignty, the state proceeds to extend its own power to imprison indefinitely a group of people without trial" (Butler 2004, 57). Essentially, Bush was accused of eroding US democracy and eroding civil liberties. Progressives were then called to uphold the law, defend US democracy, and protect civil liberties.

The question arises, however, what are we to do with the fact that, as Native scholar Luana Ross notes, genocide has never been against the law in the United States (Ross 1998, 15). On the contrary, Native genocide has been expressly sanctioned as *the law*. As legal scholar Sora Han points out, none of the post-9/11 governmental practices are actually extra-constitutional or extra-legal. In fact the US Constitution confers the right of the state to maintain itself over and above the rights of its citizenry (Han 2006). As Judith Butler has argued in her critique of "origin stories," when we critique a contemporary context through an appeal to a prior state before "the fall," we are necessarily masking power relations through the evocation of lost origins. In many even radical critiques of Bush's war on terror, the US Constitution serves as an origin story—the Constitution is the prior condition of "democracy" preceding our fall into Bush's "lawlessness." The same is true of the genocide of indigenous people; the Constitution's status as an origins story masks the genocide of indigenous peoples that is the foundation of the United States Constitution.

Native feminism provides a critical intervention in this discourse. Because the United States could not exist without the genocide of Native peoples, genocide is not a mistake or aberration of US democracy but is foundational to it. As Sandy Grande states in *Red Pedagogy*:

> The United States is a nation defined by its original sin: the genocide of American Indians....American Indian tribes are viewed as an inherent threat to the nation, poised to expose the great lies of U.S. democracy: that we are a nation of laws and not random power; that we are guided by reason and not faith; that we are governed by representation and not executive order; and finally, that we stand as a self-determined citizenry and not a kingdom of blood or aristocracy....From the perspective of American Indians, "democracy" has been wielded with impunity as the first and most virulent weapon of mass destruction. (Grande 2004, 31–32)

Thus, the nation-state, particularly the United States, is not the bastion of freedom, with some of its ideals having been eroded under the Bush regime; the policies enacted during the Bush regime in fact are the *fulfillment* of the ideals of US democracy. While the United States claims to protect the right to life, liberty, and the pursuit of happiness, all these are pursued at the expense of the Native nations that continued to be subjected to genocidal policies, the enslavement of Black peoples, and the exploitation of immigrant labor to enable this "happiness." Rather than call for upholding the law, therefore, indigenous feminism calls on progressives to work *against* the law. Thus for those committed to decolonization, the indigenous dream for America would be its end. While it seems radical to call for the end of the United States, the fact that it seems radical to call for an end to settler colonialism demonstrates the extent to which settler colonialism has so effectively limited our political imaginaries.

Rethinking Sovereignty and Nationalist Struggle

In these "postcolonial" times, terms such as sovereignty and nation have gone out of fashion within the context of cultural studies, postcolonial theory, political theory, feminist theory, and so on. Nationalism and sovereignty, it is suggested, inevitably lead to xenophobia, intolerance, factionalism, and violence. All sovereignty or nationalist struggles, it seems, are headed down that slippery slope toward the ethnic cleansing witnessed in Bosnia. Conveniently, academics who live in countries that are not being colonized, and are thus sovereign, suddenly decide that the nations that continue to be colonized and from whose colonization they continue to benefit—for example, indigenous nations—should give up their claims to nationhood and sovereignty. The assumptions behind some of these analyses are that nations are to be equated with nation-states, or that the end goal of national liberation struggles must be the attainment of a state or state-like form of governance.

The colonial context under which indigenous women live provides them an opportunity to critically interrogate the contradictions between the United States articulating itself as a democratic country while simultaneously continuing to root itself in the past and current genocide of Native peoples. If we do not presume that the United States should or will always continue to exist as a nation-state, we create the space to reflect on what exactly is a just form of governance, not only for Native peoples but also for the rest of the world. Native women activists have begun articulating spiritually based visions of nation and sovereignty that are separate from nation-states. Whereas nation-states are governed through domination and coercion, indigenous sovereignty and nationhood are predicated on interrelatedness and responsibility. These models of sovereignty are not based on a narrow definition of nation that would entail a closely bounded community and ethnic cleansing. For example, one activist distinguishes between a chauvinistic notion of "nationalism" versus a flexible notion of "sovereignty."

> To me, nationalism is saying, our way is the only right way.... [but] I think a real true sovereignty is a real, true acceptance of who and what's around you. Sovereignty is what you do and what you are to your own people within your own confines, but there is a realization and acceptance that there are others who are around you. And that happened even before the Europeans came, we knew about the Indians. We had alliances with some, and fights with some. Part of that sovereignty was that acceptance that they were there. (Smith 2008, 259–260)

This approach to sovereignty coincides with a critique of Western notions of land as property. As Patricia Monture-Angus contends, indigenous nationhood is not based on control of territory or land but on relationship with and responsibility for the land.

> Although Aboriginal Peoples maintain a close relationship with the land...it is not about control of the land...Earth is mother and she nurtures us all...it is the human race that is dependent on the earth and not vice versa...Sovereignty, when defined as my right to be responsible...requires a relationship with territory (and not a relationship based on control of that territory)....What must be understood then is that Aboriginal request to have our sovereignty respected is really a request to be responsible. I do not know of anywhere else in history where a group of people have had to fight so hard just to be responsible. (Monture-Angus 1999, 36)

It is within the realm of recognition in legal and cultural battles that Native peoples are forced to argue for their right to control to be recognized by the settler colonial state. In order to fight encroachment on their lands, indigenous peoples are forced to argue in courts that it is "their" land. What they cannot question within this system is the presumed relationship between peoples and land. That is, should land be a commodity to be controlled and owned by peoples? While arguing in the courts for "their land" might be necessary at times as a judicial strategy, it would be a mistake to presume that this is the most beneficial long-term political goal for Native peoples. As Glen Coulthard notes:

> This battle for recognition can make even Native peoples forget that they have alternative genealogies than judicial decisions for their relationship to the land, relationships based on respect for land rather than control over territory, genealogies that fundamentally question nation-state forms of governance that are premised on control, exclusivity, domination and violence. The key problem with the politics of recognition when applied to the colonial context...[is that it] rests on the problematic assumption that the flourishing of Indigenous Peoples as distinct and self-determining agents is somehow dependent on their being granted recognition and institutional accommodation from the surrounding settler-state and society....Not only will the terms of recognition tend to remain the property of those in power to grant to their inferiors in ways that they deem appropriate, but also under these conditions, the Indigenous population will often come to see their limited and structurally constrained terms of recognition granted to them as *their own*. In effect, the colonized come to *identify* with "white liberty and white justice." (Coulthard 2007)

Thus, thinking beyond "white liberty and white justice" necessarily requires a feminist analysis because the logics of heteropatriarchy fundamentally structure colonialism, white supremacy, and capitalism.

To look at how heteropatriarchy is the building block of the US empire, we can turn to the writings of the Christian Right. For example, Christian Right activist and founder of Prison Fellowship Charles Colson makes the connection between homosexuality and the nation-state in his analysis of the war on terror, explaining that one of the causes of terrorism is same-sex marriage.

> Marriage is the traditional building block of human society, intended both to unite couples and bring children into the world....There is a natural moral order for the family....The family, led by a married mother and father, is the best available structure for both child-rearing and cultural health. Marriage is not a private institution designed solely for the individual gratification of its participants. If we fail to enact a Federal Marriage Amendment, we can expect, not just more family breakdown, but also more criminals behind bars and more chaos in our streets. It's like handing moral weapons of mass destruction to those who would use America's depravity to recruit more snipers, more highjackers, and more suicide bombers.
>
> When radical Islamists see American women abusing Muslim men, as they did in the Abu Ghraib prison, and when they see news coverage of same-sex couples being "married" in U.S. towns, we make our kind of freedom abhorrent—the kind they see as a blot on Allah's creation. [We must preserve traditional marriage in order to] protect the United States from those who would use our depravity to destroy us. (Colson 2004)

The implicit assumption in this analysis is that heteropatriachy is the building block of empire. Colson is linking the well-being of the US empire to the well-being of the heteropatriarchal family. Heteropatriarchy is the logic that makes social hierarchy seem natural. Just as the patriarchs rule the family, the elites of the nation-state rule their citizens. Consequently, when colonists first came to this land they saw the necessity of instilling patriarchy in Native communities because they realized that indigenous peoples would not accept colonial domination if their own indigenous societies were not structured on the basis of social hierarchy, as was the case with many Native communities. In fact, colonists frequently complained about the lack of patriarchy within Native communities. Patriarchy in turns rests on a gender-binary system; hence, it is not a coincidence that colonizers also targeted indigenous peoples who did not fit within this binary model. In addition, gender violence is a primary tool of colonialism and white supremacy. Colonizers did not just kill off indigenous peoples in this land; Native massacres were always accompanied by sexual mutilation and rape. The goal of colonialism is not just to kill colonized peoples but to destroy their sense of being people. It is through sexual violence that a colonizing group attempts to render a colonized people as inherently rapable, their lands inherently invadable, and their resources inherently extractable.

Unfortunately, it is not only the Christian Right, but also our own progressive movements that often fail to critique heteropatriarchy. The issue is not simply how women are treated in the movement; rather, heteropatriarchy fundamentally shapes how we think of resisting and organizing in countless ways. Because we have not challenged heteropatriarchy, we have deeply internalized the notion that social hierarchy is natural and inevitable, thus undermining our ability to create movements for social change that do not replicate the structures of domination that we seek to eradicate. Whether it is the neocolonial middle managers of the nonprofit industrial complex or the revolutionary vanguard elite, the assumption is that patriarchs of any gender are required to manage and police the revolutionary family. Even feminist groups (including feminists of color) that claim to resist patriarchy often continue to work in hierarchical ways, as has been detailed in numerous women of color critiques of feminist organizing. As Rita Nakashima Brock has argued, being oppressed does not make one innocent of oppressive behavior (Brock 1995). Any liberation struggle that does not challenge heteronormativity cannot substantially challenge colonialism or white supremacy. Rather, as Cathy Cohen contends, such struggles will maintain colonialism based on a politics of secondary marginalization where the most elite classes of these groups will further their aspirations on the backs of those most marginalized within the community (Cohen 1999).

Today, indigenous and nonindigenous peoples are striving to operationalize non-heteronormative and less hierarchical visions of organizing through the process of revolution, through "trial and error." That is, rather than presume a vanguardist perspective on revolution, the philosophy behind this work is that we all need to be part of the collective process of determining how we can create a more sustainable and just world by sharing our struggles, our successes, *and* our failures. We must be committed to our long-term vision, but we must also be flexible with our strategies, understanding that our strategies will change constantly as we strive together for a more just world. Following are some specifics about working toward a different politic. These are not definitive accounts of the work being done, but some reflections on what they are trying to do, they difficulties they face, and some of the lessons that can be gleaned from their struggles. These attempts to create power do not necessarily hold "the answer" for us, but they can be conversation partners within the global struggle for social justice.

Adjoa Jones de Almeida's and Paula Rojas's contributions to *The Revolution Will Not Be Funded*, detail this organizing philosophy of "Taking Power, Making Power," that is influential in indigenous-led social movements in Latin America and is spreading among many women of color organizing groups in the United States and Canada. On one hand it is necessary to engage in oppositional politics to corporate and state power (taking power). If we only engage in the politics of taking power, we will have a tendency to replicate the hierarchical structures in our movements. Consequently, it is also important to "make power" by creating those structures within our organizations, movements, and communities that model the world we are trying to create. These "autonomous zones" can be differentiated from the projects of many groups in the United States that often try to create separatist communities based on egalitarian ideals in that people in these "making power" movements do not just create autonomous zones, but they *proliferate* them. These movements developed in reaction to the revolutionary vanguard model of organizing in Latin America that became criticized as "machismo-leninismo" models. These models were so hierarchical that in the effort to combat systems of oppression, they inadvertently re-created the same systems they were trying to replace. In addition, this model of organizing was inherently exclusivist because not everyone can take up guns and go the mountains to become revolutionaries. Women who have to care for families could particularly be excluded from such revolutionary movements. So movements across Latin America began to develop organizing models based on integrating the organizing into one's everyday life so that all people could participate. For instance, the landless movement in Brazil might organize through communal cooking, but during the cooking process, which everyone needs to do anyway in order to eat, they might educate themselves on the nature of agribusiness (Jones de Almeida 2007).

At the 2005 World Social Forum in Brazil, activists from Chiapas reported that their movement began to realize that one cannot combat militarism with more militarism because the state always has more guns. However, if movements began to build their own autonomous zones and proliferated them until they reached a mass scale, eventually there would be nothing the state's military could do. If the mass-based peoples' movements begin to live life using alternative governmental structures and stopped relying on the state, then the power of the military would become obsolete. Of course, during the process of making power, there may be skirmishes with the state, but conflict is not the primary work of these movements. And as we see these movements literally take over entire countries in Latin America, as can be seen in Bolivia, Argentina, and other countries, it is clear that it is possible to do revolutionary work on a mass scale in a manner based on radical participatory rather than representational democracy or through a revolutionary vanguard model.

Many leftists will argue that nation-states are necessary to check the power of multinational corporations or will argue that nation-states essentially are no longer important units of analysis. These groups, by contrast, recognize the importance of creating alternative forms of governance outside of a nation-state model based on principles of horizontalism. In addition, these groups are taking on multinational corporations directly. An example would be the factory movement in Argentina where workers have appropriated factories and have seized the means of production themselves. They have also developed cooperative relationships with other appropriated factories. In addition, in many factories all of the work is collectivized. For instance, a participant from a group I work with went to visit a factory; she had recently had a child and was breastfeeding. My friend tried to sign up for one of the collectively organized tasks of the factory, and was told that breastfeeding was her task. The factory recognized breastfeeding as work on par with all the other work going on in the factory.

The practice of making power then speaks to the need of building a fun revolution. I was a cofounder of "Incite!"—Women of Color Against Violence—a national organization of feminists of color who organize around the intersections of interpersonal gender violence and state violence through direct action, grassroots organizing, and critical dialogue. Organized in 2000, it currently has approximately 15 chapters and affiliates in the United States. When we began to develop our structure in 2000, we looked to a variety of organizing models for inspiration. We looked not only to groups on the Left, but also to Christian Right groups to see why they seemed to be so effective. An Incite! member attended a "Promise Keepers" rally with me as part of my academic research, and one thing we concluded was that Christian Right events were much more fun (scary politics aside!) than were events we typically attended on the Left. At the Promise Keepers rally, there was singing, comedy, sharing, and joy, whereas on the Left, we attend long, boring meetings with bad food, with everyone yelling at each other for being counterrevolutionary, and then we wonder why no one wants to join!

In that spirit, one year, instead of holding a conference, we organized a multimedia tour throughout the United States, which featured performance artists, singers, dancers, film makers, and so on, who not only gave performances but also helped community groups use arts and media as a tool for organizing. The events featured not only education, but also massage therapists, daycare, good food, and so on, and made work an act of celebration. The intent behind this kind of organizing is to build movements that engage our whole selves and give us as much as we give to the movement. What this theorizing of Native feminist activists suggests is that by starting to build the world we want to live in, we create a revolutionary movement that is sustainable over the long-term.

Thus, through the revolution of trial and error, through humility and collective sharing of mistakes and failures, we try to be part of an intellectual and organizing conversation of the future history we would like to create. As the indigenous peoples declared at the 2008 World Social Forum, when we rethink our dependence on the nation-state, we can create true democracy rather than a settler colonial politic that calls itself democracy. Rather than a pursuit of life, liberty, and happiness that depends on the death of others, we can imagine new forms of governance based on principles of mutuality, interdependence, and equality. When we do not presume that the United States should or will always continue to exist, we can begin to imagine more than a kinder, gentler settler state founded on genocide and slavery.

References

Brock, Rita Nakashima. 1995. "Ending Innocence and Nurturing Willfulness." In *Violence Against Women and Children: A Christian Theological Sourcebook*, edited by Carol Adams and Marie Fortune. New York: Continuum, 71–91.

Butler, Judith. 2004. *Precarious Life*. London: Verso.

Cohen, Kathy. 1999. *The Boundaries of Blackness*. Chicago: University of Chicago Press.

Colson, Charles. 2004. "Societal Suicide." *Christianity Today* 48:72.

Colson, Charles, and Anne Morse. 2004. "The Moral Home Front." *Christianity Today* 48:152.

Coulthard, Glen. 2007. "Indigenous Peoples and the 'Politics of Recognition' in Colonial Contexts." Paper presented at the Cultural Studies Now Conference. University of East London, July 22.

Grande, Sandy. 2004. *Red Pedagogy*. Lanham, MD: Rowman and Littlefield.

Han, Sora. 2006. "Bonds of Representation: Vision, Race and Law in Post-Civil Rights America." Santa Cruz: University of California-Santa Cruz.

Jones de Almeida, Adjoa. 2007. "Radical Social Change." In *The Revolution Will Not Be Funded*, edited by Incite! Women of Color Against Violence. Cambridge: South End Press, 187–195.

Monture-Angus, Patricia. 1999. *Journeying Forward*. Halifax: Fernwood Publishing.

Rojas, Paula. 2007. "Are the Cops in Our Heads and Hearts?" In *The Revolution Will Not Be Funded*, edited by Incite! Women of Color Against Violence. Cambridge: South End Press, 197–214.

Ross, Luana. 1998. *Inventing the Savage: The Social Construction of Native American Criminality*. Austin: University of Texas Press.

Smith, Andrea. 2008. *Native Americans and the Christian Right: The Gendered Politics of Unlikely Alliances*. Durham, NC: Duke University Press.

CHAPTER 2

Race, Religion, and the Pursuit of Happiness

James H. Evans Jr.

We hold these truths to be self-evident,
that all men are created equal,
that they are endowed by their Creator
with certain unalienable Rights
that among these are
Life, Liberty and the pursuit of Happiness.

The Declaration of Independence guarantees that all persons under its purview are entitled to the pursuit of happiness. It does not promise that this happiness will necessarily be achieved, but that to pursue it is an inalienable right. This promise is funded by the "social contract" that exists among free and equal persons. This contract does not define happiness per se, but its application to collective life in the United States suggests that there are three major trajectories to happiness. Ironically, these same trajectories had to be framed in a manner that excluded people of African and Native American descent as participants in the national conversation, while demanding that they submit to the authority of that contract. Life and liberty are construed as foundational to the pursuit of happiness for free and equal persons.

For those who are thought to be neither free nor equal, the meaning of life and liberty has been shaped by the notions of race and religion. For African Americans, Latinas/os, and Native Americans the meaning of life is contextually framed by the dynamics of race. Whether one seeks to embrace race and racialized ethnicity as a symbol of pride or to reject them as categories that limit the expression of one's humanity, race and racialized ethnicities are continually a force to be reckoned with. Specifically for African Americans, to speak about life on an individual or collective level means to engage, at some level, racial discourse. Likewise, the notion of liberty for African Americans is framed with the context of religious discourse. Part of the reason for this is that the idea of a separation between the religious and the sociopolitical dimensions of life are foreign to the African mindset. Another and perhaps more important reason for this connection is that liberty is seen as not only as the political privilege of the powerful, but also as a divine gift and inheritance. African American thinkers from Frederick Douglass to Henry Highland Garnet have understood liberty in theological and political terms. Frederick Douglass, a great abolitionist orator in the nineteenth century, spoke of this American notion of liberty as a divine right granted to all people by their creator. Henry Highland Garnet was a nineteenth-century African American writer who spoke of this American notion of liberty in connection with an understanding of freedom as the essence of what it means to be human. The issue here is not the separation of church and state, but the spiritual basis for apprehending material reality. Even Dr. Martin Luther King Jr.'s brilliant oratory did not only argue for the liberty of Black folk on the basis of the Constitution or the Declaration of Independence, but framed the argument in terms of a deeper spiritual reality, namely, the equality of all people in the eyes of God. One way to get at the connection between one's understanding of life and its meaning and one's understanding of liberty and its meaning, is to see them against the backdrop of race and religion. Through these lenses, the notion of the pursuit of happiness should also be refracted. The central question is "How is happiness pursued (and defined) in the context of exclusion and denigration of one's personhood?" There are three arguments for the exclusion of Black people from the social contract that protects the pursuit of happiness (Allen and Pope 2006). The first suggests that the social contract was an arrangement that had no place for African Americans. The second suggests that the social contract was for the benefit and protection of the powerful. Since African Americans had no political power, they were excluded from the benefits of such a contract. The third argument suggests that the social contract reflected a divine mandate of sorts. This meant that the exclusion of African Americans from this contract was a matter of divine providence. I want to suggest that an examination of these arguments can shed some light on the problems and possibilities for the pursuit of happiness today, not only for the poor and oppressed among us, but also for the community as a whole.

Race, Religion, and the Economy of Happiness

When considered in light of our racial history, the notion of happiness is defined and experienced within a specific "economy." That is, happiness is experienced in the context of a specific and concrete social arrangement. The Declaration of Independence proffers its promise of life, liberty, and the pursuit of happiness that is to be guaranteed by the Constitution. These documents are the written expression of the "social contract" that binds together free and responsible citizens. However, for African Americans this social contract has been experienced as a "whites only" contract. The exclusion from this contract has been based on race and justified by religion. Further, this experience of not being included in the social contract has yielded an understanding of happiness that is severely restricted.

The national narrative of freedom in the United States has been interpreted to promise a place for any person willing to work hard and contribute to the common good. This narrative was the basis of the attractiveness of the United States to European immigrants in the early twentieth century. However, this same national narrative intentionally and consciously excluded enslaved Africans and their descendants in America. This exclusion was based not simply on race, but on a specific conception of race. In this context, race was the marker of the displaced and misplaced. The Dred Scott Decision of 1857 that asserted that the Black man had no rights that a white man was bound to respect, excluded Black people from exercising the rights promised to participants in the social contract. The Fugitive Slave Law of 1850 de facto meant that every state in the union was a slave state. This law allowed any slave owner to pursue his property even into those states where slavery had been abolished. Even free Blacks could be apprehended and held until they produced proof of their status as free. Thus, there was no place where a Black person could live free from the risk of capture and enslavement. Black people were excluded because they were not seen as consenting participants in the social contract. Ironically, however, they were bound to the terms of that contract with or without their consent. That is, the enforcement of the provisions of the contract applied to them as well. Thus, race became a marker for determining who had a place in the national conversation and who did not. This exclusion was based on race, but was justified by religion.

The national narrative was also supported by religion, and, importantly, a particular religious understanding. Then, as now, the nature of that religious understanding was the subject of debate. In this instance, the religious views of Thomas Jefferson were perhaps as influential as any. Jefferson understood religion to be the rational expression of Deism. Deism affirms that while God created the universe, God remains at a distance from the same, allowing or mandating that humanity take responsibility for the management of it. In a deistic view, the place of God is marginal to any social arrangement. It is not surprising, then, that Jefferson is credited with coining the phrase "the separation of church and state," which is simply a corollary of the separation between God and the world. Religion for Jefferson is based on reason rather than revelation; religion is the rational expression of Deism. In essence, this view of religion argues for a specific and limited place for the divine in the human economy. This deistic God, withdrawn and seemingly disinterested, left a vacuum in the human economy that was filled by American patriarchalism.

Patriarchalism has a long and varied history in Western political thought originating in Aristotle's linking of familial structures with political authority. That is, one should obey political authority as one obeyed the patriarch (father) of the household. Even Martin Luther linked the commandment to "honor thy father and thy mother" with the obligation to submit to royal authority. (Oddly enough, subsequent iterations of this idea left out "thy mother"). Although Jefferson and other American revolutionaries rejected the authority of the monarchy, they did not reject, in principle, patriarchalism. The American Revolution resulted in the rejection of the church as the presence of God on earth, the symbol of divine paternalism, and the crown as the unquestioned authority and the single human embodiment of patriarchalism. However, patriarchalism found a new, more subtle and durable expression in Republican principles, and representative forms of government. Theism suggested that God was directly involved in human affairs through the divine authority of the church or the political authority of the crown or both. Thus, the marginalization of the church as a symbol of divine authority and the disposition of the crown as the symbol of human authority, both tied as they were to a theistic notion of God, could only be accomplished with a deistic God. In this gap, a secular patriarchalism appeared.

The claim that supports any patriarchal arrangement is that it provides the best chance for the happiness of all. But what is the nature of this happiness? In this context, happiness is marked by stability and order. In a situation of inequality, this happiness is only maintained by asserting that this inequality is normal. (A corollary to this idea is that slavery is normal). To put it in contemporary terms, happiness, in this patriarchal context, is dependent on maintaining economic inequality. The contemporary relevance of this understanding now becomes clear. Too often, in America today, happiness is associated with reaping the lion's share of benefits from the prevailing economy.

Race, Religion, and the Politics of Happiness

Beyond the economic order, happiness is also defined within the context of a concrete political arrangement. As idealistic and lofty as their language might be, the Declaration of Independence and the Constitution recognize that human communities are by nature political communities. That is, while an appeal to reason is necessary, it is not sufficient to the creation and government of the commonwealth that these documents envision. Not only does enlightened self-interest hold communities together; power also plays a role in creating community. The national narrative, then, is not only idealistic, it is also political. That narrative not only tells the story of the triumph of great ideas, but also, albeit in muted tones, of the power dynamics that make those ideas dominant. Thus, the social contract that provided the basic plot of the national narrative included provisions for the equitable distribution of power and limited exercise thereof. The social contract provided for the protection of individual property (the idea that such property was private, as such, came later) because the possession of such property was itself a necessary sign of the power to participate in the national narrative. Recall that the right to vote was originally granted only to propertied men. In other places as well, the recognition that the commonwealth needed more than high-sounding rhetoric to hold it together was evident. In this view, ideas are important, but power is indispensable. Enslaved Africans and their descendants were historically denied this power. The exercise of the power of the ballot was blocked, frustrated, and denied to Black people. The denial of the vote to Black people was, again, based on a certain conception of race. One way to justify this exclusion was to claim a natural inferiority for Black people. They were seen as not having the intelligence, or the skill, or the courage to resist slavery.

Thomas Hobbes, a dour architect of the national narrative, argued that nature was fundamentally a state of war. In the natural realm, there is fierce, life and death competition, the victors get the spoils, and the vanquished are put to death. The only way to rise above a state of nature in which life is "solitary, poor, nasty, brutish and short" is the selection of a sovereign with the absolute power to keep order. In this view, the essence of the social contract is the voluntary submission to the sovereign. Human nature does not change, as people are still prone to all-out war. That nature is contained and restricted, but does not change. In nature, the victors and the vanquished are clearly identified and, in Hobbes's view, locked in an unending struggle for survival or dominance. Therefore, he proposed that only the selection of an absolute sovereign could prevent a complete collapse into barbarism. One of the most powerful justifications for the enslavement of Africans was that they were by nature destined to be submissive and servants. This natural destiny of slavery also meant that Black people could not, as a matter of principle, voluntarily submit to such a sovereign. Race became a sign of political powerlessness. Black people, in this context, could not exercise the power to vote because they could not own property. They could not own property because they were property. Race became a marker of the vanquished in this natural war. Because the victors had the right to exterminate the vanquished due to their natural deficiencies, slavery arguably represented a just limitation on the power of the victors.

This view of the enslaved African as the vanquished enemy in war (although one would be hard pressed to identify the actual war that was waged) is supported by a Hobbesian view of religion. For Hobbes, nature was the state of war, and religion was the moral expression of the laws of nature. Hobbes had difficulty holding together his view of nature as war and any traditional view of God. Thus, rightly or wrongly, he is identified as an atheist. To be fair, in Hobbes's era atheism did not refer to the absence of belief in God, but to the absence of belief in providence (Hobbes 1651, especially chapter 31). Hobbes often denied the charge that he did not believe in God, but functionally, God was not necessary in his universe. In this context, his religion simply acknowledged that the world is ruled by the powerful, and this functional atheism made room for the notion of American supremacy based on power. The claim that supports any supremacist political arrangement is that the happiness of the powerful is all that matters. What is the nature of this happiness? In this context, happiness is marked by power and dominance. In a situation where there are significant power differentials, such happiness is justified by the claim that it is natural. (A corollary to this idea is that slavery is natural.) To put this point in contemporary terms, happiness is associated with the security that results from the disproportionate exercise of power. The contemporary relevance of this view now comes into focus. Happiness in America today is too often dependent on the powerful maintaining a competitive advantage over the powerless.

Race, Religion, and the Morality of Happiness

There is a third dimension to the pursuit of happiness that remains to be discussed. Happiness in this context is more than economic benefit or political spoils. It is viewed as right and just. Here the iron clad structure of the economy of happiness and the jagged edges of the politics of happiness are hidden beneath the conciliatory sheath of the morality of happiness. The national narrative of the United States does not claim legitimacy solely based on its economic or political dimensions. It claims a moral basis for its legitimacy. The social contract between free and equal persons cannot be, in the final analysis, sustained by its ideas or its reflection of the distribution of power. There must be a sense that it is just and right, that is, it is moral. This morality has a deeply emotional component to it, but does not rest on any appeal to emotion. It appeals to reason. While the emotional component is not built into the documents that fund the national narrative of the United States, the reception or reading of that narrative is often accompanied by an emotional response.

This response is most clearly seen in the conversations and controversies surrounding the national flag and the national anthem. Alteration, desecration, or distortions of these national symbols can elicit deeply emotional responses. Jimmy Hendricks's rendition of the national anthem was remarkable and controversial because it reflected an alternative reading of the national narrative. Instead of the predictable and measured chords, his rendering emphasized the discord and conflict embodied in the narrative. Or one could point to the Olympic protests of 1968, when Tommie Smith and John Carlos, winners of the gold and bronze medals, respectively, in Mexico City held up their fisted right hands with black gloves as the US national anthem was played. Around the world the image of this "silent gesture" was seen as a promotion of Black Power. Among other things, the Black Power Movement sought to provide an alternate reading of the national narrative—one that asserted that the oppression of Black people was neither normal nor natural. The protests of these two athletes were seen as objectionable not only because they symbolized an alternative reading of the national narrative, but also because they, too, elicited an emotional response. What has been most often overlooked is that Tommie Smith states in his autobiography that the protest was not a Black Power protest but a human rights protest. They were wearing Olympic Project for Human Rights badges at the time (Smith 2007). Black Power was seen as a more vital threat to the national narrative than the campaign for human rights.

In its moral manifestation, the social contract made race an indisputable mark of identity. One's race and one's identity were one and the same. One's ethnicity was related to one's ethos or the moral sphere in which one lived. Religion, then, supported this morality. John Locke described true religion as the toleration of difference (Locke 1689). For Locke, religion had to be tolerant, because religious tolerance was the corollary to the triumph of reason. Locke claimed that humanity had been given reason and, along with it, a law that cannot contradict reason. The reasonableness of Christianity, in this context, was held in contradiction with its approval of slavery. Since the irrationality of slavery did not invalidate the reasonableness of Christianity, the social contract that excluded Black people was justified by the claim that slavery was providential (it is God's will because it is reasonable to us) and American exceptionalism (the view that America's manifest destiny is to rule).

In this context what is happiness? Happiness is marked by the enjoyment of hegemonic privilege that is justified by fate or providence. Therefore, happiness in America is associated with the moral assurance that one deserves what one has. One can see this in the curious claim by some wealthy persons that, all evidence to the contrary notwithstanding, they deserved their riches. This claim of deserving or merit is a moral claim that finally relieves one from guilt.

Conclusion

What if happiness is more than the acquisition of material surplus? What if happiness is more than hegemonic influence over "others"? What if happiness is more than pseudo-consent to fate and providence? The Declaration of Independence grants us the right to pursue happiness but does not tell the definition of happiness. Perhaps, what is needed is a national conversation about happiness—not an attempt to fantasize about having more but a consideration of what makes us happy. This conversation must include persons for whom happiness has been an elusive goal. For most Black folk, happiness has to be wrested from the struggles of everyday life. Although this is true for other racial-ethnic minorities as well as for many other Americans—many more than those who want to admit it—there is something crucial to be learned from the experience of African Americans. Perhaps there is something even more desirable than happiness per se. What about joy? One definition of joy, according to the Encarta World English Dictionary, is "great happiness: feelings of great happiness or pleasure, especially of an elevated or spiritual kind." While it is likely that the framers of the Declaration of Independence thought that the pursuit of happiness was the chief human aim, it is possible that they set their sights too low. I want to suggest that it is not just happiness that should be the object of our pursuit, but great happiness, or joy. The saints of the African American faith understood this as they rarely, if ever, spoke of happiness without also speaking of joy. When they spoke of their ideal state, they declared that there was "joy and happiness there, in My Father's House." The durability of joy as they understood it was expressed in the claim that "This joy that I have, the world didn't give it to me. The world didn't give it, the world can't take it away." This is why although the Declaration of Independence permits the pursuit of happiness, African American Christians and others have insisted on more than individual freedom and moved toward communal joy.

Joy differs from happiness in both degree and kind. Happiness can be an individual achievement and experienced as an inward feeling of satisfaction. But when that satisfaction rises to the level of joy, its boundaries are expanded. It becomes so much more than what can be materially acquired. When that happiness becomes great, it also becomes joy. This joy elevates our passions and reveals its source in moments of spiritual elevation. This joy cannot always find expression in words. It is often, as Barbara Holmes notes, an "unspeakable joy." This does not mean that it is inarticulate, but that its greatest expression is often seen in silent acts of solidarity.

The 2012 Presidential Election and the Pursuit of Happiness

During the primary season before the recent presidential election, the struggle within the Republican Party to select a candidate revealed a deep fissure. On one hand many Republican evangelical Christians resolutely affirmed that only an evangelical Christian candidate would be acceptable to them. The eventual selection of Mormon Mitt Romney with nary a complaint from the Religious Right was made palatable because Governor Romney would give his silent support to the escalating racial rhetoric from these religious groups. It became clear that Romney's religion was no barrier to receiving the support of the Religious

Right. Their ability to accept Romney was not based on their suddenly acquired tolerance of religious diversity, but in the fact that Romney represented their best chance of removing an African American president from office. In essence, race trumped religion. However, there was another aspect of the selection of Governor Romney that should not be overlooked. The Christian Right whose political aims were to establish a kind of theocracy in the United States, joined forces with the super wealthy whose political aims were to establish a kind of plutocracy in the United States. The assumption was that theocrats and plutocrats, separately, had little chance of winning. But together they could redirect American society. In an pernicious rhetorical synergy, the public scorn for people of color from the theocrats coalesced with the public ridicule of "the poor" from the plutocrats. In America, "the poor" often means Black people and Latinos. This unholy alliance, ultimately, proved to be no match for a hopeful and determined electorate. What the election should have taught us is that a communal vision will trump racial vitriol. President Obama modeled forward looking and optimistic leadership. The outcome of this election should remind us that hope, not fear, is the human default position. It is this fear that obscured the fundamental nature of the pursuit of happiness, or even joy, in our lives. An important lesson to be taken from the 2012 presidential election is that happiness is elusive when it is connected to racial intolerance or rapacious greed. But the right to seek it is an inalienable right.

References

Allen, Anita L. and Thaddeus Pope. 2006. "Social Contract Theory, Slavery, and the Antebellum Courts." In *A Companion to African American Philosophy*, edited by Tommy L. Lott and John P. Pittman, 125–133. Malden, MA: Blackwell.

Hobbes, Thomas. 1651. *Leviathan or The Matter, Forme and Power of a Common-Wealth Ecclesiastical and Civill*. Available at http://www.gutenberg.org/files/3207/3207-h/3207-h.htm.

Locke, John. 1689. *A Letter Concerning Toleration*. Available at http://etext.lib.virginia.edu/toc/modeng/public/LocTole.html.

Smith, Tommie. 2007. *Silent Gesture: The Autobiography of Tommie Smith*. Philadelphia, PA: Temple University Press.

Tippett, Krista. 2010. "Summit on Happiness." From the NPR show *On Being*. Available at http://cslr.law.emory.edu/news/news-story/headline/krista-tippett-on-being-radio-airs-happiness-summit/.

CHAPTER 3

pax americana, pax humana

Sharon Welch

Who are we as Americans?[1] What is our role now on the world stage? What are the best means of supporting the "ideals of liberty, self-determination, and equality in the rule of law"? In two speeches, both delivered in 2009 a few days apart, President Barack Obama announced a new foreign policy that signals the possibility of a momentous shift in US thinking about the nature of power, the limits of force, and the complexity of building peace and preventing conflict (Obama 2009a and 2009b). His remarks are part of a widespread and substantive debate among political theorists and political leaders about the foundations of international order itself, and the legitimate and essential role of the United States in fostering international peace and stability.

Robert Kagan, senior associate at the Carnegie Endowment for International Peace, Jean Bethke Elshtain, professor of social and political ethics, and Niall Ferguson, professor of history, all urge the United States to accept responsibility as the guarantors of European and American security, international order, and freedom (Kagan 2003; Elshtain 2003, 6–7, 169–170; Ferguson 2003, 367–370). Jonathan Schell, noted journalist, and Zbigniew Brzezinski, national security advisor under President Carter, propose another path, asking us to be "liberal internationalists," applying "cooperative power" to the "international sphere" (Schell 2003, 265; Brzezinski 2004, vii, 4, 18, 135–138, 217–218). Like William Schulz, former executive director of Amnesty International USA, they encourage the United States to shape, with other nations, a new "international society," responsive to the "common enemy of terrorism," and resolutely committed to human rights and global justice (Schulz 2003, 211, 152).

Which path will we follow? We may try to become the beneficent guardians of "peace, prosperity and liberty" envisioned in the 2002 National Security Strategy of the Bush administration, preferring alliances but willing to act alone (Bush 2002). Or, we may become the "multilateralists" envisioned by President Barack Obama and the political theorist Joseph Nye Jr., as skilled in the exercise of persuasive cultural and political power as we are judicious in the use of economic and military might (Nye 2003; Obama 2009b).

We live in a time rife with debates about the best use of our national power, debates that hinge on understandings of the very nature of national and international power, and on interpretations of colonial history. William Schulz, for example, warns against imperialism and asks that we remember that moralistic domination breeds "resentment, resistance, and rebellion" (Schulz 2003, 61). Niall Ferguson takes quite a different lesson from the undeniable brutality yet seemingly irreplaceable achievements of the British Empire and asks the United States to resolutely accept the challenges of establishing and maintaining a Pax Americana (Ferguson 2003, xii, 367–370).

Many people within the United States acknowledge and embrace the thrill of Empire—the intoxication of mastery, the security of being met with deference if not respect, the challenge of assuming the mantle of destiny, of shaping the world in our image. The National Security Strategy of the United States of America reflects these goals. In its preface, President Bush states, "The United States enjoys a position of unparalleled military strength and great economic and political influence." The document defends "a distinctly American internationalism" in which the United States will retain military supremacy and will use its influence to spread "freedom, democracy and free enterprise." (Bush 2002) Those who would be the bearers of Empire most often see themselves as the harbingers of security and peace. From the order of the Pax Romana, through the "civilizing" global reach of the British Empire, to the freedom, democracy, and prosperity promised by imperial America, the rhythms of power, of truth, of unassailable military might, of absolute security swirl, surround, and overwhelm.

There is, however, a different rhythm in the widespread dissatisfaction with the US military actions in Iraq and Afghanistan. There are voices throughout the world calling for other ways of maintaining order and security, other means of bringing tyrants to justice, other forms of power, vitality, glory, and community. President Barack Obama, Jonathan Schell, William Schulz, Zbigniew Brzezinski, and Joseph Nye Jr. are among those who urge the United States to become something that we have not yet fully been—a shaper, with other nations, of a cooperative international order that can set limits to the excesses of any imperial power, ours included. As Obama stated bluntly in his Nobel Peace Prize acceptance speech:

> I believe that all nations—strong and weak alike—must adhere to standards that govern the use of force. I—like any head of state—reserve the right to act unilaterally if necessary to defend my nation. Nevertheless, I am convinced that adhering to standards strengthens those who do, and isolates—and weakens—those who don't. . . . America—in fact, no nation—can insist that others follow the rules of the road if we refuse to follow them ourselves (Obama 2009b).

Robert Kagan, in his influential book *Of Paradise and Power,* derides the vision of a cooperative rule of law as the perennial resort of the weak. He advocates another vital role for the United States: the guarantor, through military supremacy, of global order—the power that is necessary for "paradise." While European nations may choose international law over military struggle, Kagan, like Jean Bethke Elshtain, claims that there are other nations and peoples not so restrained, and some power must be ready to meet the challenges they pose with "military might" (Kagan 2003, 13, 28–29, 37, 55–57, 73–74, 86–87).

A similar logic was expressed by the framers of the 2002 National Security Strategy of the United States. The writers of the document acknowledged that "coordination with European allies and international institutions is essential for constructive conflict mediation and successful peace operations." The reach of these cooperative activities, however, was seen to be sharply limited: the serious threats of brutal leaders and global terrorism require military action and may necessitate even preemptive, unilateral action by the United States. "The greater the threat, the greater is the risk of inaction—and the more compelling the case for taking anticipatory action to defend ourselves" (Bush 2002, 11, 14).

The divide here is clear. Many people believe genuine power and decisive action require unilateral military force. Others, however, claim that coercive military force can be counterproductive—that we can, as Schulz states, in our defense of our power lose it. Schulz argues that if we violate the human rights of opponents and dissidents in our defense of national and international security, we lose not only moral integrity but also political viability (Schulz 2003, 60–64, 212). The divide, through, is greater than a mere debate about the relative utility or folly of military intervention in particular situations. Kagan and the writers of the National Security Strategy fail to recognize that what is being proposed by other political leaders and scholars is not a strategy of the weak, not a form of inaction in the face of grave threats, but another vision of world community and of the ways peoples and governments can exercise power responsibly in the face of grave threats and great opportunities.

Again, the words and actions of President Obama are instructive. In his Nobel Peace Prize speech he articulated the ideal of cooperative action, limited by international norms: "America's commitment to global security will never waiver. But in a world in which threats are more diffuse, and missions more complex, America cannot act alone" (Obama 2009b). In the case of Libya, these values were put to the test. Obama and others saw the threat of crimes against humanity as stark as those in Rwanda and Bosnia, and chose to act preemptively: "As President, I refused to wait for the images of slaughter and mass graves before taking action." Significantly, the action taken was multilateral, a cooperative international response to appeals from the Libyan opposition and the Arab League. Obama clearly defined the responsibility of the United States: "Our task is . . . to mobilize the international community for collective action. . . . American leadership is not simply a matter of going it alone and bearing all of the burden ourselves. Real leadership creates the conditions and coalitions for others to act as well. . . . To see that the principles of justice and human dignity are upheld by all" (Obama 2011).

Such momentous choices, so starkly delineated in dualistic terms: imperial America or international cooperation, power or paradise, coercive power or cooperative power, hegemony or survival (Chomsky 2003). To set the debate in these terms misses the creative claims that are being made by many critics of imperial and colonial power. The alternative to the domination of the many by a single unassailable military power is neither isolationism nor a refusal of global responsibility. It is, rather, a third way, another definition of strength and power, and a different way of using and limiting military force.

Some political leaders and theorists continue to advocate unilateral power and American exceptionalism. Niall Ferguson, for example, explicitly advocates that the United States assume the mantle of empire. It is, however, noteworthy that this same rhetoric is not commonly found within the United States itself. Although many people certainly advocate an exercise of power that can arguably be called imperial in its ambition, range, and scope, few explicitly advocate an American Empire. The Bush administration, for example, repeatedly denied that the US military presence in Iraq was an occupation. Patrick Tyler, writing for *The New York Times*, cited the words of Paul Bremer as he assumed charge of United States operations in Iraq: "We are not here as colonial power. . . . We are here to turn over [power to the Iraqi people] as quickly as possible" (Tyler 2003).

Why does "imperial America" sound like a critique of the hubris of the United States rather than the nonideological description of a laudable goal? In this disjunction—comfort with the unilateral use of power, yet distaste for the name of "empire"—lies great potential and great peril. To simply dismiss this disjunction as the greatest hypocrisy is to miss a creative tension, one that, if fully explored, can lead us to a more just expression of who we are, as a people, as a nation, and as members of an international community.

We may continue to wield overweening power, blinded by our own desires for purity and beneficence to the costs of that power, unwilling to acknowledge resistance to dominance and unwilling to see and mourn the catastrophic consequences in human suffering and death. We may, however, choose another path, taking hold of that tension, exploring it honestly, and building from that prescient discomfort a different expression of national and international power, one as creatively attuned to our weaknesses and limitation as to our strengths.

What is it about *who* we are and *where* we are that leads to these tensions? We need to understand the urge to use military power and to act unilaterally. At the same time, we must not ignore the continued reluctance to claim unabashedly the role of imperial America. We may, as a nation, courageously acknowledge our complex history as Americans and propose a vision of national power that is rooted in the best of our values and aspirations as well as in the worst of our excesses and brutality. And, far from being utopian, this is a vision that is eminently pragmatic. Remember the etymology of utopia—literally, "no-place." What could follow is a vision of national identity and global responsibility that emerges from this place—from the Hawaiian islands to the mainland to Puerto Rico—and from this people—indigenous Americans and the continuing flow of immigrants, voluntary and involuntary, from Africa, Europe, Latin America, and Asia—who make this place their home, their culture, and our nation.

This is a vision that also emerges from our encounters with other places, with other peoples, with other stories. It emerges as we learn from "others"—others who are not beneficiaries of Empire, but those who bear its costs. Seeing this vision requires learning from peoples who have different views of community, power, national identity, and global responsibility (as further explored by Welch 2004).

Seeing the World through the Eyes of Others

Seeing difference is a learned art—and an essential task. Learning to hear fundamental critiques of our actions and to critically assess alternative views of human community and of ethical and political responsibility is the task of global citizenship and global ethics. This is also the task of postcolonial comparative religious ethics.

After spending time in a Zen temple, the French philosopher Michel Foucault offered an assessment of the "turning point" in European thought occasioned by the end of imperialism. He claimed that the philosophy of the future would "be born outside of Europe or equally born in consequence of meetings and impact between Europe and non-Europe" (Foucault 1999). What Foucault predicted for philosophy has come true in the comparative study of religion.

The very category of "religion" emerged as a result of European contact with other religious systems (Chidester 1996; Long 1986). While colonialists were engaged in significant military conflict, they claimed that the indigenous peoples they attacked had no religion, and, were, therefore, practically subhuman. Seen by the invaders as barriers to the march of civilization, they could be removed, even exterminated. Chidester recounts the case of southern Africa where colonialists saw the resistant population as having peculiar "customs" but lacking religion. But once the indigenous populations were subjugated, those same "customs" were then taken as evidence of religion—a religion, however, that was customarily misunderstood in two ways. On the one hand, it was falsely described as ahistorical and uniform (significant differences between peoples and changes throughout time were dismissed as inconsequential). On the other hand, it was often characterized as a primitive or degenerate form of monotheism. Well into the twentieth century, the traditions of non-Europeans were seen as "other," sometimes in an ostensibly positive sense as an exotic reality to be explored and appreciated, more often in a negative sense, misunderstood as fundamentally irrational and childishly superstitious (Dean ed. 1995). The use of material objects in religious rituals and ceremonies, for example, while taken for granted as valid in the Christian reverence for the cross and the use of bread and wine in religious ceremonies, was described pejoratively as the use of fetishes in other than Christian religions (Brown 1991).

Contact among religious traditions is now taking a radically different form in the postcolonial era. By "postcolonial," activists and scholars refer to a political situation in which the process of colonization (economic, cultural, and political conquest) is both contested and relatively visible. The term does *not* mean that domination has disappeared. While many of the colonial powers in Africa and the Americas have been defeated, the process of political, economic, cultural, and military domination continues in other forms. Ania Loomba provides a thorough discussion of the complexities of postcolonial studies, analyzing the difficulties with the term *postcolonial* itself. Not only may it imply that domination has ceased, but we run the danger of missing the different forms of colonialism and of resistance to colonialism; we also run the danger of missing the different ways in which aspects of "precolonial" culture continued to exist even during colonization. She argues, however, that "the word 'postcolonial' is useful in indicating a general process with some shared features across the globe. But if it is uprooted from specific locations, 'postcoloniality' cannot be meaningfully investigated, and instead, the term begins to obscure the very relations of domination that it seeks to uncover." Loomba agrees with Jorge de Alva, who defines postcolonialism "not just as coming literally after colonialism and signifying its demise, but more flexibly as the contestation of colonial domination and the legacies of colonialism. Such a position would allow us to include people geographically displaced by colonialism such as African-Americans or people of Asian or Caribbean origin in Britain as 'postcolonial subjects' although they live within metropolitan cultures. It also allows us to incorporate the history of anti-colonial resistance with contemporary resistances to imperialism and to dominant Western culture" (Loomba 1998, 12, 19).[2]

A critique of colonial reason is well established in the field of religious studies and has led to proliferation of works that describe patterns of misunderstanding and misnaming in regard to particular religious traditions.[3] This critique helps us see more clearly both the past and present contours of exploitation and domination. These critiques recover previously neglected historical materials: the critiques of European and Euro-American colonization by indigenous peoples. If we pay attention to those voices, what we find is a sharp critique, expressed in incredulous laughter, and in searing pain. While the beliefs and habits of the European and Euro-American conquerors often seemed ludicrous, their cruelty and domination was heartrending and unfathomable. Indigenous peoples of the Americas knew warfare, but they were stunned by the massacres of whole villages by Europeans, and by the deliberate mutilation of those who resisted forced labor or conversion (Wilson 1998). These voices, historical and contemporary, also express different vision of power, community, and global responsibility.

What Foucault claimed as true about epistemes is also true about ethics and politics: we need differences to see injustices that are fundamental, and constitutive of a political, ethical, or religious system. As we listen to these critiques of our interactions with other peoples, as we study histories other than our own, we find that there are compelling ethical and aesthetic alternatives to imperial power.

Our Peace Mandate

Niall Ferguson argues that the real question is not *whether* Empire but *whose* Empire, and claims that a Pax Americana would be preferable to that of any other (Ferguson 2003, 358–370). With Kagan, he is in a long line of historians, political leaders, and even theologians who see Empire as the inevitable expression of genuine power, the natural outflow of military and moral strength. While there are many who see Empire as desirable, and even more who see Empire as inevitable, there are others who can imagine a variety of constellations of national and international power and order. This alternative to Empire is neither inevitable nor free of risk and cost. It is, however, an adventure that is, ironically, as pragmatic as it is audacious.

Let us think for a moment about the challenge posed in President Obama's Nobel Peace Prize address, the injunction "to think in new ways about the notions of just war and the imperatives of just peace." Obama acknowledged the limitations and dangers of military intervention, dangers that are intrinsic to war itself: "The instruments of war do have a role in preserving the peace. And yet this truth coexists with another—that no matter how justified, war promises human tragedy. . . . war itself is never glorious, and we must never trumpet it as such" (Obama 2009b).

He went on to explore alternative forms of political power, and advocated three ways of building a just and lasting peace:

- Alternatives to violence tough enough to change the behavior of political leaders and governments;

- A just peace based on the inherent worth and dignity of every individual;
- A just peace that encompasses economic security and opportunity (Obama 2009b).

Although many people throughout the world find this vision of a just, cooperative, international order compelling, it would be the utmost folly to deny the attraction of Empire. Empire attracts, yet Empire also repels. I invite us as global citizens to a celebration, an invocation, and an exaltation of the logic that both knows the intoxication of Empire and yet confronts the costs of imperial power. This is an invocation of these capacities of heart and mind that enable us to see the costs of Empire, a celebration of other plays of energy, power, and vitality—the exuberance of other ways of being as peoples and as nations.

Finally, this vision is a wager. Although he resisted the power of the emerging Third Reich, the great twentieth-century theologian Paul Tillich wrote that history lives under the star of Empire (Tillich 1967, 339–342). We, however, may celebrate other stars and invoke, with gratitude and wonder, their continued presence—stars of reverence, of compassion, of virtuosity, honesty, curiosity, and respect. Viable alternatives to imperial power are no less assured than is the inevitability of some form of political, economic, and military domination. Is history under the star of Empire? Can humans move from the rule of law inside nations to the rule of law between nations? These questions cannot be answered in advance of the doing. They are wagers to be lived, risks to be taken, not conundrums to be resolved in theory.

One thing, though, is certain. If we as citizens of the United States are to discover a peace mandate, it will not be a simple repetition of the mandates of other peoples. Our peace mandate will come from our history, from our stories, and from our open engagement with other peoples, other nations, and other visions of community and power. Our peace mandate simultaneously emerges from and transforms who we are as individuals, as political activists, as a nation, and as global citizens. Such a mandate reflects and recasts our personal stories of belonging, hope, and fear; it reflects and recasts our deepest ethical and spiritual commitments. Our peace mandate emerges from our collective history as citizens of the United States and our collective vision of who we have been and of who we may become as citizens in a global community. As we learn to see differently the complexity of our individual and collective histories and tradition, we may find the resources that enable us to take up the task of global citizenship, with honesty, daring, and creativity.

Notes

1. This essay is a revised version of the preface in my previous book (Welch 2004) and is used with permission. In regard to my use of the term "American," it is important to note that many people are critical of the use of the term America to refer to the United States. The term is, of course, incorrect, taking as it does the name of an entire continent for the name of one nation within that continent. In *Terrible Honesty*, Ann Douglas writes of the period in the 1920's when the term was widely adopted by people in the United States: "The nation was usually referred to not as the 'United States,' but as 'America'...Americans in the 1920's liked the term...precisely for its imperial suggestions of an intoxicating and irresistible identity windswept into coherence by the momentum of destiny" (Douglas 1995, 3). Given that such an imperial identity is now the subject of debate, it seems fitting to use the term in this context.
2. See also the works of Fanon 1963, 1991; Achebe 2001; Bhabha 1994; Said 1978; Spivak 1999.
3. See also Long 1986; Brown 1991; Chidester 1996; and Deloria Jr. 1992, 1999.

References

Achebe, Chinua. 2001. "An Image of Africa: Racism in Conrad's *Heart of Darkness*." In the *Norton Anthology of Theory and Criticism*, edited by Vincent B. Leitch, 1783–1794. New York: Norton.

Bhabha, Homi K. 1994. *The Location of Culture*. London: Routledge.

Brown, Karen McCarthy. 1991. *Mama Lola: A Vodou Priestess in Brooklyn*. Berkeley: University of California Press.

Brzezinski, Zbigniew. 2004. *The Choice: Global Domination or Global Leadership*. New York: Basic Books.

Bush, George W. 2002. *The National Security Strategy of the United States of America*. Available at http://georgewbush-whitehouse.archives.gov/nsc/nss/2002/.

Chidester, David. 1996. *Savage Systems: Colonialism and Comparative Religion in Southern Africa*. Charlottesville: University Press of Virginia.

Chomsky, Noam. 2003. *Hegemony or Survival: America's Quest for Global Dominance*. New York: Henry Holt.

Dean, Thomas, ed. 1995. *Religious Pluralism and Truth: Essays on Cross-Cultural Philosophy of Religion*. Albany: State University of New York Press.

Deloria, Vine Jr. 1992. *God Is Red: A Native View of Religion*. Golden, CO: Fulcrum.

Deloria, Vine Jr. 1999. *Spirit and Reason: The Vine Deloria, Jr. Reader*. Golden, CO: Fulcrum.

Douglas, Ann. 1995. *Terrible Honesty: Mongrel Manhattan in the 1920s.* New York: Farrar, Straus, and Giroux.

Elshtain, Jean Bethke. 2003. *Just War against Terror: The Burden of American Power in a Violent World.* New York: Basic Books

Fanon, Frantz. 1963. *The Wretched of the Earth.* New York: Grove.

Fanon, Frantz. 1991. *Black Skin, White Masks.* New York: Grove.

Ferguson, Niall. 2003. *Empire: The Rise and Demise of the British World Order and the Lessons for Global Power.* New York: Basic Books.

Foucault Michel. 1999. "Michel Foucault and Zen: A Stay in a Zen Temple." In *Religion and Culture*, edited by Jeremy R. Carrette. New York: Routledge.

Kagan, Robert. 2003. *Of Paradise and Power: America and Europe in the New World Order.* New York: Knopf.

Long, Charles H. 1986. *Significations: Signs, Symbols and Images in the Interpretation of Religion.* Philadelphia: Fortress Press.

Loomba, Ania. 1998. *Colonialism/Postcolonialism.* London: Routledge.

Nye, Joseph Jr. 2003. "U.S. Power and Strategy after Iraq." *Foreign Affairs* 82.4: 65–69.

Obama, Barack. 2009a. "Remarks by the President to the Nation on the Way Forward in Afghanistan and Pakistan." December 1. Available at http://www.whitehouse.gov/the-press-office/remarks-president-address-nation-way-forward-afghanistan-and-pakistan.

Obama, Barack. 2009b. "Remarks of the U.S. President in Oslo." December 10. Available at http://www.nbcnews.com/id/34360743/ns/politics-white_house/prin#.Uelul42Th8E

Obama, Barack. 2011. "Obama's Speech on Libya (Text)." *The New York Times*, February 23.

Said, Edward W. 1978. *Orientalism.* New York: Pantheon.

Schell, Jonathan. 2003. *The Unconquerable World: Power, Nonviolence and the Will of the People.* New York: Henry Holt.

Schulz, William F. 2003. *Tainted Legacy: 9/11 and the Ruin of Human Rights.* New York: Nation Books.

Spivak, Gayatri Chakrovorty. 1999. *A Critique of Postcolonial Reason: Toward a History of the Vanishing Present.* Cambridge, MA: Harvard University Press.

Tillich, Paul. 1967. *Systematic Theology, Three Volumes in One. Vol. 3. Life and the Spirit: History and the Kingdom of God.* Chicago: University of Chicago Press.

Tyler, Patrick. 2003. "New Overseer Arrives in Baghdad in Sudden Revision of Top Positions by Washington." *The New York Times*, May 13.

Welch, Sharon. 2004. *After Empire: The Art and Ethos of Enduring Peace.* Minneapolis, MN: Fortress Press.

Wilson, James. 1998. *The Earth Shall Weep: A History of Native America.* New York: Grove.

PART II

Creative Practices that Emerge from
Lo Cotidiano (*The Everyday*)

CHAPTER 4

The United States as a Responsible Member of the Global Community: Life, Liberty, and the Pursuit of Happiness When Globalized Militarization Matters

Keun-Joo Christine Pae

It has been almost ten years since I first visited Rainbow Center, a New York City-based nonprofit organization for ex–US military brides from South Korea who used to work in the sex industry for American military servicemen. I still remember the conversation that I had with Jenny (pseudonym) and Reverend Henna Han, the founder of the center. After having divorced her violent and alcoholic husband, a former American GI in Korea, Jenny, a drug addict at that time, walked into the Rainbow Center. "She looked like a hobo" said Rev. Han. "I asked her why she came here. She said, 'I want to live life like other people do.' So, I asked her back, 'What do you mean?' Then, Jenny looked at me as if she couldn't believe my question. She said, 'You are a pastor and do not know what it means to live life? I want to eat when other people eat. I want to go to bed at night when other people sleep, go to work in the morning when other people do. Everyone, even a woman like myself, has the right to live." As Rev. Henna Han recalled her first meeting with Jenny, Jenny was smiling and saying, "Thanks to Rainbow Center, I was able to live like other people do. I overcame drug addiction and now have a job good enough to support myself."

Since the meeting with Rev. Han and Jenny, my theological contemplation has revolved around the meanings of human life in various contexts. According to the Christian confirmation of human life, we, humans, are created in the image of God and therefore our life is sacred. However, the notion of this sacrality often excludes the lives of millions of women like Jenny, who had to sexually cater to American soldiers abroad for mere economic gain.

Having lived in both the United States and South Korea, I often wonder how many Americans know their political decisions affect many people like Jenny beyond US territory. This is why right after transmitting President Obama's Union Address in 2012, the Korean media immediately read between the lines of the address, assuming the US impact on the Korean economy and national security in relation to North Korea's possible possession of nuclear weapons. While most Americans focus on the United States' own liberty and happiness, Washington DC affects the lives of millions people in Korea, Iraq, Chile, and with broad global significance. In the case of Jenny, her sexual labor for American soldiers in Korea and migration to the United States through marriage were the results of US foreign policy.

It is not an exaggeration to say that all Americans have dual citizenship—American and global. When they vote, Americans do not influence only domestic political, economic, and social structures; their votes also have consequences at the global level. How will our exercise of liberty and pursuit of happiness look, if we seriously consider our global citizenship as God's call to take responsibility for all Her/His creation? What ethical decisions can we make, if we take the sacrality of US military sex workers' lives into seriously theological consideration? Emphasizing the dual citizenship of Americans, I would like to invite readers to contemplate these questions, especially focusing on why Americans should pursue happiness, keeping in mind the global impact of our decisions at home. I would like to propose that American readers engage this essay with a listening attitude so that they will further critically reflect on their ethical responsibility for life.

Mapping Out America's Global Responsibility for Life, Liberty, and the Pursuit of Happiness

There is no doubt that the United States is the world's utmost superpower. In spite of the current deep recession, its economic and military power surpasses that of any other country. At the same time, the ever-interconnected world, through excessive globalization, forces the

United States to cooperate with other countries for global security and peace. Globalization happens not only through trade or tourism, but also through the increasing militarization of the world. During the Cold War period, excessive militarization, including in the Asia-Pacific region, was justified by appealing to the need for a balance of power between communism and free-market democracy. In the twenty-first century, this need no longer exists. The United States, the only military superpower in our time, and many other countries militarized during the Cold War continue to exist and are responsible for numerous armed conflicts and for the race to have weapons of mass destruction. This global reality forces us to think about how to create a strategic plan for global security and peacebuilding that would overcome militarization and its impact on ordinary people's lives. In other words, we need to think about security and peacebuilding worldwide in our attempt to reinterpret the meaning of life, liberty, and pursuit of happiness in the United States.

Security and peace are the fundamental grounds for human life. As Simone Weil emphasizes, "security is an essential need of the soul" (Weil 2007, 32). Security means that the soul is not under the weight of fear or terror, "except as the result of an accidental conjunction of circumstances and for brief and exceptional periods" (32–33). If we, as Christians, want to pursue happiness, we need a secure ground for our physical and spiritual well-being in order to live fully, as Jesus of Nazareth promised. Excessive militarization of the world, in fact, threatens our physical and spiritual security, and thus prevents us from living fully. In order to understand the impact of excessive militarization on our lives, liberty, and pursuit of happiness, we need to learn about the brutality of transnational militarism and experiences like that of Jenny. Then, we can audaciously and creatively build lasting peace and security as the grounds for all human beings to pursue meaningful lives and happiness.

As a Christian feminist ethicist whose primary concern is global peacemaking, I use gender and sexuality as tools in analyzing globalized militarism, especially the transnational presence of the US armed forces. My research has focused on how militarism has been globalized through the process of heterosexist patriarchal modern nation-building, and how transnational US militarism has affected gender relations in a country like South Korea that has hosted this foreign army for more than six decades. Growing up in South Korea, I was constantly reminded by the US military's presence that I lived in a war zone. I was aware of this as well as another burdensome reality, that of militarized prostitution: the Recreation and Relaxation business (so-called R&R) for US soldiers across South Korea. The stories of Korean women working in the Recreation and Relaxation business give a vivid picture of what life is like in the context of globalized militarism.

Particularities of Military Prostitution

During the Korean and Vietnam Wars, the Recreation and Relaxation business was systemically constructed and maintained by the national governments and the US military in Asian countries such as the Philippines, Thailand, Japan, and South Korea. It is no secret that sex industries are "ubiquitous around the military bases" and that soldiers have used women sexually "through rape, kidnapping, and slave brothels that follow armies" (Brock and Thistlethwaite 1996, xix). The International Criminal Tribunal for the former Yugoslavia made the global community aware of how systemic rape and forced prostitution have been used frequently as a military tactic in modern warfare. However, commercialized military prostitution is somewhat detached from the ethical discourse concerning military crimes and violence because it is considered a business that engages voluntary sex workers. The exploitation of these sex workers is considered more a problem of global capitalism than of global militarization.

On the contrary, feminist international political thinker Cynthia Enloe argues that military prostitution is not a separate issue from military rape. The patriarchal assumption that soldiers have uncontrollable sexual drives leads politicians to seek ways of providing for them safe and commercialized sex. For it allows the soldiers to avoid being accused of military rape and thus evades creating diplomatic conflicts (Enloe 2004, 121). Male politicians, the majority in international politics, secretly look for safe and commercialized sex in order to satiate male soldiers' sexual desires, to keep up military morale, and to avoid anti-American sentiments due to military rape where American soldiers are stationed (125, 149). It is a fact that military prostitution policies have a long history in US international politics (Enloe 2008, 51). This reality has not changed in spite of women's increasing participation in politics, because international politics is still considered a male domain, mainly because it requires difficult military decisions.

The development of US military prostitution in South Korea supports Enloe's feminist analysis of international politics. Since Korea's independence from imperial Japan in 1945, US armed forces have been stationed in South Korea. The United States–Korean military relationship was strengthened through the Korean War (1950–1953) followed by the United States–Korea Mutual Defense Treaty known as SOFA. By the end of 1945, a few months after the arrival of the US military in South Korea, Bu-Pyung, a small town between Seoul and Inchon, became the first camptown where American soldiers stationed at Inchon sought out liquor and women for recreation. Since then, camptown prostitution has evolved in different stages: the early stage (1945–1949), the foundation of the Recreation and Relaxation business (1950s), the golden days (1960s), the systematic corporation (1970s to mid-1980s), and the declining period (mid-1980s to the present). These stages correspond to the number of American soldiers stationed in South Korea, changes in American foreign policy, and the economic development of South Korea (Moon 1997, 27–32).

In 1957, the South Korean Ministry of Public Health and the US Eighth Army first gathered Korean military prostitutes at geographically marked places in order to control venereal diseases (Yi 2004, 232–233). Park Jung-Hee's military regime in the 1970s more actively controlled Korean military prostitutes through the Camptown Clean-up Campaign. In 1969, the Nixon Doctrine initiated the withdrawal of twenty thousand American soldiers from South Korea by March 1971. The Park administration regarded the reduction of the United States military forces as a risk for national security. In order to prevent further reduction of American soldiers, the Korean government modernized camptowns and effectively controlled Korean military prostitutes. Korean prostitutes who worked at bars and clubs for American soldiers had to have regular medical check-ups at the government-funded clinics. Those who were declared clean of venereal disease could obtain VD cards as the official sanction to sell their bodies. All military prostitutes had to be registered with the local police station and wear name tags while working at the bars and clubs. Once a month, governmental educators gathered sex workers in order to indoctrinate them with the idea that their service for American soldiers was crucial for peace and security (Moon 1997, 104–126).

With the Korean state pimping sex workers through programs like the Camptown Clean-up Campaign, women—consciously or unconsciously—were recruited into the state war project, just as soldiers are recruited into a particular war or military duty. For this reason, the liberal feminist argument supporting women's autonomy to choose sex work as their profession fails to adequately address the state violence that perpetuates military prostitution. Similarly, the Marxist-Leninist emphasis on exploitation does not uncover the heterosexist patriarchal ideology behind military prostitution. US military prostitution in South Korea should be analyzed through the lens of military and state violence or even wartime violation of human rights. More precisely, we need to analyze how Americans are consciously or unconsciously involved in military prostitution that suppresses poor women's liberty and hinders them from pursuing happiness. We further need to analyze what responsibility the transnationally stationed US forces should take for human life, liberty, and happiness.

Reminding the readers of this essay to think of it as a listening project, I now share some stories that I collected during field research at Sunlit Center for elderly sex workers in Anjungri of Pyeong Taek, Korea, the camptown set up for entertaining American soldiers, which is adjacent to Camp Humphreys. These stories help us to consider what global peacebuilding means and how we in the United States are all called to protect all human life, to exercise liberty without harming others, and to pave a way for the pursuit of happiness of all persons.

Sunlit Center: The Narratives of Military Brutality and Political Apathy

Located in Anjungri of Pyong Taek, Kyeong-Gi-Do, a Southern satellite city of Seoul, Sunlit Center serves the role of advocating for elderly women who used to sexually cater to American GIs. In the summer of 2011, I had the opportunity to observe Choong-ang University and Sunlit Center's joint project to collect the narratives of elderly women, who spent most their lives in one camptown after another. As a participant observer, I was allowed to attend the group meetings. Although it is impossible to generalize particular stories from the women at Sunlit Center, here, I highlight three perspectives from these women's narratives, which may reveal why the oppression caused by military prostitution should be analyzed in terms of violation of human rights, and thus inform an alternative understanding of peacebuilding for the protection of sacred human life.

First, Sunlit Center's elderly women are aware of the Korean government's and the United States military's involvement in camptown prostitution through VD cards, military curfew, and education about reproductive health, legal marriage, and so on. Some women's narratives also indicate that American soldiers' misbehavior and arrogance stemmed from the triangular relationship between the United States, South Korea, and North Korea. One elderly woman narrates, "When drunk, soldiers yelled at us, 'We are here to protect you from North

Korean communists. In return, you should serve us well.'" The women's stories often describe their lives caught between the United States and South Korea or American men and Koreans. They suffered mistreatment from Korean bar owners, pimps, and from American soldiers, which was understood to result from Korea's lack of military and economic power. An analysis of these women's narratives raises further questions about the moral justification of the American military's presence in South Korea.

Second, many of the women's narratives indicate that both the Korean government and the US military are unwilling to protect sex workers from violence and exploitation in camptowns. As a result, the workers are exposed to consistent physical, sexual, and psychological violence, and are often caught in the fights between soldiers. In the group meeting, several women said that some soldiers fought over them, but that when the police arrived, the women themselves were blamed for the fight. After the soldiers' fights, some women were not allowed to work. Laughing, one woman said, "GIs can go crazy. They shoot, fight, drink, and sleep with women. What can we expect? They are soldiers." Raped and physically attacked by GI customers or by club owners, sex workers can hardly expect law enforcement agents to protect them or to punish the perpetrators. Military prostitutes are treated as criminals in South Korea, where prostitution is illegal, and the United States–Korean Mutual Defense Treaty does not give the Korean authority power to investigate GI crime, unless the perpetrator is caught when the crime physically happens. In fact, many war crimes against humanity, such as systemic rape and sexual slavery, happen when the state is incapable or unwilling to protect the victims or when the state denies the occurrence of sexual crimes against women.

Third, some narratives exemplify how the absence of a social safety net after a brutal war can harm women for an indefinite period. The various postwar statistics in Africa and in Asia show the increase of diverse forms of male violence against women. For instance, K, a woman in her sixties, entered military prostitution at age 16 after having been sexually abused at an orphanage. As a Korean War orphan without a birth certificate, K was unable to obtain a citizenship card. The club owners took advantage of her status by charging her for a fake identification card and stealing her cash savings. According to K, one Native American soldier wanted to marry her. After his one-year-duty in Korea, he had to go back to the United States but sent her money and the legal documents needed for marriage. However, without her citizenship card, she could not prepare immigration documents. One year later when the man came back, he misunderstood the situation and thought that K did not want to marry him. In his sorrow, he shot himself. Telling her story, K expressed her love-and-hate relationship with the United States and South Korea—not with the American soldiers.

Anjungri is the last stop for many military sex workers. When a US military base is relocated or closed, military prostitutes move to another camptown, work at brothels for Korean soldiers, Korean customers, or foreign tourists, or migrate to foreign countries, including Japan, Australia, and the United States. A camptown like Anjungri is the only place where they feel less stigmatized as bad women, and military prostitution is the only job they know how to do. This is why the elderly women I met at Sunlit Center had spent most of their lives in the military sex industry.

Spiritual Activism: Life, Liberty, and the Pursuit of Happiness in the Era of Globalized Militarism

Globalized militarism has drastically militarized women's life on a global level. Furthermore, militarization as a transformative process of society has changed American culture steadily and continuously. For example, since September 11, publicly criticizing the American military has been widely viewed as an unpatriotic act, as an act of disloyalty (Enloe 2004, 146). As a result, it becomes harder and harder to publicly reveal male-on-male or male-on-female sexual violence within the US military, and American soldiers' sexual engagement with local men and women in the countries like Iraq, Afghanistan, and Japan, to name only a few. More and more American colleges accept ROTC programs and research weapons of mass destruction. Whether aware or unaware, all Americans live in an excessively militarized culture and often consider militarization as a way of life.

In this militarized culture, what alternative ways to pursue a meaningful human life and happiness can we envision? My field research at Sunlit Center further leads me to imagine transnational spiritual activism with an emphasis on political and spiritual resistance of globalized militarism and the search for a peacemaking project beyond disarmament. Spiritual activism focuses on the mystery of human life; liberty in accordance with the life of Jesus, the Prince of Peace; and the meanings of happiness that embrace the global human community.

What I mean by transnational spiritual activism is threefold in relation to life, liberty, and the pursuit of happiness. First, increasing global interconnectedness and interdependence challenge any peacemakers to search for global networking, even though their work is grounded in their local communities and their perspectives on war and militarization are diverse. In other words, many peace activists are keenly aware that one country's armed conflict globally affects people's lives. Several local organizations in South Korea, including Sunlit Center, Du Re Bang (My Sister's Place), Safe Korea, and Women Making Peace create networking among themselves, while actively seeking global solidarity with other antimilitary organizations such as Women for Genuine Security in San Francisco Bay Area, Gabriella in the Philippines, and Women Act against Military Violence in Okinawa. Through international conferences and the internet, these organizations share their peacebuilding strategies and information about the US military's impact on women's lives, and support each other's political activism. Together, they continue to make known how military forces are not being held accountable for global security or peace. For these organizations, peacebuilding is not merely the absence of armed conflict, because war against women's bodies does not end when war comes to an end. Furthermore, the militarization of a society often increasingly happens after war.

Aiming at the physical and spiritual transformation of militarized culture, peacebuilding must involve reclaiming the sacrality of all human life, exercising civil liberty to resist militarism, and pursuing happiness in a nonviolent way. This needs the recognition that globalized militarism, especially in the Asia-Pacific region, began with Japanese imperialism, followed by American imperialism. Imperialism has been fed by false beliefs that the lives of people of color are less important than those of civilized whites; that women's lives can be used to strengthen a country's military and economic power; that liberty can be secured through ownership of natural resources and the labor power of the subjugated; that material possession is the source of happiness; and that my happiness always precedes others' happiness. Peacebuilding through spiritual activism must first show how these false beliefs have destroyed meaningful human relations nurtured by love and compassion. Recovering love-and-compassion-based human relations has to be part of the process of articulating and practicing true liberty and pursuit of happiness.

Second, military prostitution suggests the need for a robust and critical analysis of globalized militarism and international politics through the lens of gender and sexuality. This analysis would offer alternative perspectives on the meanings of life, liberty, and pursuit of happiness. When I asked Soon-Duk Woo, the executive director of Sunlit Center, for the meaning of peace, she answered, "Peace means each of these elderly women is respected and treated as a human being in society. That each one can have three bowls of warm steamed rice everyday and does not worry about dying alone." Woo's understanding of peace is similar to Jenny's dream of living life the way others do. And her vision of peace further suggests that international politics must be informed and analyzed through the impact they have on women's everyday life and human relations. In fact, the analysis and transformation of women's everyday life is as important as the so-called big picture in international politics, such as nuclear policy or military deployment. Every aspect of international politics and military policy is about everyday human relations. When mainstream discourse on international politics dismisses the importance of everyday human life, we must resist this form of knowledge production. For instance, Korean sex workers in US military camptowns have been silenced for the sake of security and peace because mainstream peace discourse has narrowly focused on the disarmament of North Korea and the reunification of the two Koreas, rather than taking into account ordinary citizens' everyday lives.

Hence, we need to address how US foreign policy can take ordinary citizens' everyday lives into consideration. First of all, we need to resist the division between track-one diplomacy, which is played by elite politicians, and track-two diplomacy, of which the main players are nonprofit organizations, including religious ones. Although the importance of track-two diplomacy is ever increasing, the final military decision is in the hands of track-one diplomacy. Track-one diplomacy often resists the information from the raw stories of women and men whose lives are threatened by military violence. Therefore, we must demand that our politicians listen to ordinary people closely so their stories are taken into account before they make political decisions. They need to ask themselves the following questions: (1) How will a certain decision secure an ordinary citizen's right to nutrition or physical security? (2) How will this decision affect gender relations locally and globally? and (3) How will a particular political decision bring happiness into human lives locally and globally? Assessing political decisions through the eyes of the downtrodden such as Korean sex workers who serve American military servicemen is difficult, but not impossible.

From a Christian perspective, Jesus can be a role model for the politicians. Jesus named himself as the Prince of Peace. As the Prince of Peace, he did not play in the big picture of international politics, but spent time with the downtrodden. Jesus listened to the sick, prostitutes, tax collectors, and sinners, while religious and political authorities did not communicate with them. Since Jesus was physically present with the downtrodden, he could value the life of lepers, recognize the seed of peace in Galilean fishermen, preach the radical vision of the kin-dom of God, and continue to inspire peacemakers to fight against colonial oppression even after his death. Jesus's life teaches us that international politics can protect human life and liberty only when it is grounded in ordinary people's everyday life.

Finally, I draw spiritual activism from Christian mysticism. Dorothee Sölle articulates mysticism as a power for the resistance of violence, militarism, status quo, political apathy to suffering, and so on. For Sölle, deep contemplation on the sacrality of life or living in mystical union with God turns the triviality of everyday life into wonder, joy, and astonishment (Sölle 2001, 88–93). This mystical experience leads one to empathetically embrace others' suffering and sustains one's life in the midst of darkness, confusion, and exhaustion (146–155). Christian spiritual practice is not an isolated or individualized event. Neither does it concern only spiritual salvation. Rather, Christian spirituality leads one to appreciate the web of life created by God and sustained by God's love. Christian spirituality makes it possible for us to see ourselves as part of the web of life.

Liberty for Christians must move around the genuine appreciation of the web of life. Just as St. Ignatius's prayer says that "*Suscipe, Domine, universam meam libertatem*" (Receive, O Lord, all my liberty), so we, as Christians, have to exercise our liberty in accordance to God's love for the world. Liberty is not unregulated actions or accumulation of private property. Neither is happiness. From a Christian perspective, liberty emerges when we are willing to live life responsibly before God and Her/His creation. Happiness arises when we live harmoniously with God's creation. Only then will we experience the interconnectedness among all God's creation, and fully embrace the sacred dwelling in every form of life. This experience is not metaphysical but one that takes place in our world and our lives today.

Conclusion: Living Beyond the Fear

Meditating on what I experienced at Sunlit Center leads me to conclude that spirituality makes it possible to develop a creative and audacious activism that counters globalized militarism, while at the same time revealing new meanings of life, liberty, and the pursuit of happiness. To engage in this kind of spirituality, American citizens must educate themselves to the fact that US militarism builds multiple walls, such as that between military prostitutes and good women, American soldiers and local Koreans, and allegedly patriotic Americans and non-patriotic peace activists. These walls prevent us from pursuing meaningful human relations of love and compassion. Furthermore, militarism separates the soldier's body from the mind through military training, and creates apathy toward those who are suffering from military violence. Spirituality as resistance would help overcome these multilayered separations. Deep meditation on humanity may also lead scholars and activists to avoid self-righteous certainty concerning military projects or women's development because it allows us to see both good and evil inside us and empowers us to use our liberty to choose good over evil in spite of our brokenness.

One might question which comes first, American citizenship or global citizenship. Although global citizenship is still difficult for many of us to conceptualize, there can hardly be a separation between the two. For instance, during every season of presidential elections, at least four issues are repetitively argued by the presidential candidates: women's reproductive rights, the security of the American economy, America's ongoing wars abroad, and immigration. All these issues, in fact, are global issues. Just as some conservative politicians who read the Christian Bible with a gender biased view attempt to regulate women's bodies and sexualities, the US military controls Korean sex-workers' bodies through VD clinics—not for the reproductive health of these women but to ensure healthy military morale. There is a connection between political attempts to regulate women's bodies in the United States and in South Korea. We should remind ourselves that what is happening in the United States affects many outside the country as well. Hence, we must continue to inquire about what America is doing in global countries and whether America truly protects human life and liberty.

Finally, we must face the fear that feeds the militarization of the world. After having researched 91 women's grassroots organizations against militarism across the world, the British sociologist Cynthia Cockburn invites her readers to imagine "one individual who can reveal how the coercive power relations of class, race and gender intersect so as to shape life and changes, and to exemplify what war has to do with this" (Cockburn 2007, 257). What Cockburn sees from where this imagined woman stands is that "the struggle no longer seems to be against war itself, or rather not against war alone . . . [but] goes beyond even the positive search for peace. It's a project of liberation . . . from fear" (258). Cockburn's words resonate with Christian peacemakers' mantra: The

Spirit of God is not the spirit of fear, but the spirit of freedom, justice, and love. Let us not fear but choose life over death, use our liberty to exorcize fear in the militarized culture, and pursue happiness embracing the global community.

The Declaration of Independence assures us that life, liberty, and the pursuit of happiness are the fundamental rights of human beings. Are Americans ready to accept that these fundamental rights should be shared among all global citizens?

References

Brock, Rita Nakashima and Susan Brooke Thistlethwaite. 1996. *Casting Stones: Prostitution in Asia and in the United States.* Minneapolis, MN: Augsburg Fortress Press.

Cockburn, Cynthia. 2007. *From Where We Stand: War, Women's Activism, and Feminist Analysis.* New York: Zed Books.

Enloe, Cynthia. 2004. *The Curious Feminist: Searching for Women in a New Age of Empire.* Berkeley and Los Angeles, CA: University of California Press.

———. 2008. *Manuevers: The International Politics of Militarizing Women's Lives.* Berkeley and Los Angeles, CA: University of California Press.

Moon, Katherine H. S. 1997. *Sex among Allies: Military Prostitution in U.S.—Korea Relations.* New York: Columbia University Press.

Sölle, Dorothee. 2001. *Silent Cry: Mysticism and Resistance.* Minneapolis, MN: Fortress Press.

Weil, Simone. 2007. *The Need for Roots.* Translated by Arthur Wills. London and New York: Routledge.

Yi, Yim Hwa. 2004. *Korean War and Gender.* Seoul, Korea: Seo Hae Mun Jip.

CHAPTER 5

Living Sustainably toward Social Justice: Asceticism Revisited

Paula M. Cooey

C an a person live a life of self-denial in the service of others and enjoy it? Is such a life liberating? Does this life require withdrawal from this world or rejection of it? A growing number of people would answer a resounding "yes" to the first two questions and an emphatic "no" to the second one, which begs a further question: How does a life of self-denial free a person, bringing joy in the process? How does a life of self-denial square with the pursuit of happiness?

Life, liberty, and the pursuit of happiness: isn't this precisely what The Declaration of Independence assures us "all men" a right according to human nature? The history of this assurance is ambiguous, because the original "men" were restricted to white landowners and slave owners. There are additional ambiguities as well. Are these rights strictly individual or are they communal in some sense? And, what is a right? Does it entail an obligation? Is life restricted to biological life or is a certain quality involved? Liberty from what and for what? Who gets to define happiness and for whom? Independent from what and for what? The specifics remain enticingly absent, perhaps to prod us to fill them in for any given time, place, and generation as we go in response to the times in which we live.

In this time and place, one of the most pressing issues that current generations face is environmental devastation culminating especially in global climate change. For those who accept global climate change as a given, the disaster consequent from First-World habits of production and consumption call for a reorientation of desire that re-habituates humankind to lives freed from excessive material attachments that produce a never-ending need to consume. Obesity, disease, waste, poverty, and the irreparable damage to the natural environment on which these habits depend belie the satisfaction promised by material gain. A reorientation, by contrast, entails a generosity of the good and goods with the rest of life on the planet, both human and non-human, in other words, a commitment to social justice beyond wants, needs, and benefits characteristic of present practices.

In response, many individuals and communities have turned to sustainable living as an alternative. The work of living sustainably, or leaving as little a carbon footprint as possible (using as little carbon-based energy as possible) while working for justice for others, has long been in play among a number of communities, religious and secular alike. At the same time, such engagements are far from having caught on as a mass movement, partly because of the dreariness often associated with the kind of self-denial that this lifestyle appears to involve. People may associate repression, moralism, and grimness with asceticism. They often associate lack of humor, joy, and individual imagination with such reform. People may likewise associate gorging, unrestrained license, and unchecked individualism with liberty and happiness. For those who agree with the values of restraint and service and who want to reject excess, however, contemporary ascetics question how to avoid the negativity and world rejection mistakenly identified with the self-denial that these values require.

I suggest that sustainable living toward social justice calls for a new asceticism that will potentially liberate us in ways that make us happier. By new asceticism I mean denying ourselves material good that waste natural resources that grow ever scarcer or face extinction. For example, my family assumed that eating three meat-centered meals a day was necessary to a good diet. We now know that this practice is not only not necessary, it is also not healthy, and it depends on practices that involve unjust treatment of labor in some cases, engage in animal cruelty in some, and threaten the continued flourishing of whole species in other cases. We can reduce our meat intake in ways that could, because of the values this reduction represents, make us happier (not to mention healthier). Because valuable land may either return to its natural habitat or be freed up for much needed production of grains and vegetables for an indigenous population, this particular practice of self-denial becomes an act of generosity. To make my case, I will briefly and selectively explore some stereotypical assumptions surrounding asceticism before turning to two religious communities that exemplify what I would describe as an asceticism characterized markedly by the happiness and generosity of its various members toward others outside the respective communities.

Stereotypes of Asceticism vs. A More Adequate Theory

Popular stereotypes of asceticism, as well as early scholarship on the subject, presuppose a model grounded in the naturalization of desire and its repression. The ascetic performs acts of self-denial that include, among other things, celibacy and intentional poverty, commitments that appear as a rejection of normal desires grounded in bodily needs. These acts also may involve what many regard as bodily mutilation to induce pain as a cleansing mechanism of the natural lusts of the will. The ascetic may engage in such behaviors in solitude or may join a community, usually religious, of like-minded ascetics who have well-developed formal practices of self-denial. In either case, the practices of self-denial appear to the outsider to stand as a rejection of this world, often through a separation from it. In short, this common conception pathologizes ascetic practices and ascetics: surely nobody in his or her right mind would devote a lifetime to self-denial. After all, hunger and sexual desire are part of human nature, in need of channeling, perhaps, but denied only at great risk to the psyche. Likewise, poverty should be avoided at all costs in preference for a life of material comfort.

While asceticism in its most extreme forms may seem at the very least troubling to the modern mind, this view fails to recognize its own secularized ascetic practices (take the rigor of athletic or artistic training, the self-denial involved in a careerist work ethic, for example). Nor does this view realize the learned behavior involved in its own excesses (to what extent are we taught to want what we want?). It equally runs afoul of current scholarship on ascetic phenomena and ascetics. The model of desire the modern mind assumes, the model's presuppositions about what pain does or does not accomplish, its *laissez faire* capitalist view of intentional poverty, and a cultural inattention to history are simply in error. The stereotyped view of asceticism is insupportable, given what social scientists now know about desire and what historians have learned about asceticism (Wimbush and Valantasis 1998). This popular view ignores the socioeconomic implications of desire as well. Not understanding this mistake has serious consequences for the future.

The word *asceticism*, from the Greek, *askesis*, simply means training. The practices that ascetic training involves historically range from small self-sacrifices to major ones, often having to do with a denial of appetite or desire. Training is often connected to bodily functions (hunger) or bodily parts (inflicting anything from mild discomfort to serious pain). Ascetic practices could include anything from the trivial—giving up chocolate for Lent—to the more profound and demanding—becoming a leader of a nonviolent rebellion. Notable ascetics include prophets like Jeremiah and John the Baptist from the remote past to Dorothy Day and Mohandas Gandhi from the comparatively recent past.

As for desire, scholars now know that it is fluid in both its exercises and its objects (Valantasis et al., 2006; Wimbush and Valantasis 1998; Foucault 1990). Our understanding of our own needs and wants as well as the objects of those desires, sexual and otherwise, are subject to manipulation even to the point of reconstruction, taught formally and informally from cultural and countercultural cues. Desire's pursuits, as well as its goals or objects, repeated over and over, become habitual. In other words, there isn't a fixed something called "desire" that preexists its objects and its needs or wants; rather, the disciplining of wants and needs is active in the production of desire itself. By "wants" I mean quite simply things we can do without, for example, iPhones, or designer clothes; by "needs" I mean things, phenomena, and people upon which we depend in order to survive, for example, food, air, and human nurture. Advertisers would often have us believe that a want is a necessity. We are taught our excessive desires as well as their self-denial. (Whether the process is "successful" is another story, as any educator or Madison Avenue CEO can attest.) In respect to the building of habits or training required to establish self-denial, scholars also know that the line between pain and pleasure is at best blurred (Scarry 1985); intentional self-inflicted pain, under certain conditions, can produce pleasure by releasing endorphins into the brain (athletic practices like jogging come to mind as a secular example). These chemicals of the brain produce euphoria or happiness. Of equal importance, social scientists and historians have learned that what appears as a moral, social, or economic practice regarding wants and needs of a minority group in one context may well be absorbed into its dominant culture as a norm at a later point in history. For example, religious freedom was once seen as not only a "want," but also a heretical one; now it is seen as a necessity to democratic life in the United States

Two examples will suffice to illustrate ascetic practices that produce freedom and happiness—Anabaptists from sixteenth-century Europe and a Roman Catholic women's religious community in the United States, the Sisters of St. Joseph of Carondelet from the present. Both communities have required of their members a simple life according to what is understood by each to be the principles set forth by the Gospels. Living according to these principles has required ascetic training of the participants to habits not yet normative in dominant cultures from which they have emerged. In the case of the Anabaptists, in spite of the odds against their survival, they continue to exist today, with their historical legacy of a certain kind of freedom now absorbed into the present dominant culture as its ideal, if not always its actuality. In regard to the Sisters, their practices illustrate their asceticism as a source of happiness or joy. How such habits became and continue to become second nature in ways that produce freedom and happiness provides my central focus. The following example of the Anabaptists has less to do with happiness and more to do with freedom. My point here is to show that a minority culture's values—in this case simple living and freedom of conscience— can transform into dominant cultural norms. The Sisters of St. Joseph of Carondelet exemplify how practices of self-denial lead to happiness.

Sixteenth-Century Anabaptists

Why focus on sixteenth-century Anabaptists? The sixteenth century marks a time of extreme violence, from the European global expansion beginning in 1492 through the Wars of Religion that spilled over into the seventeenth century. Waves of plague, repeated unsuccessful revolutions by peasants, threats of a Muslim conquest of Europe, and the internal corruption and debauchery of the royalty and upper classes characterized the era. Notwithstanding humanism and the beauty it produced, the shoulders on which humanist culture stood included the political intrigue and warmongering among the royalty, severe family dysfunction among the elite patrons, the moral bankruptcy of the Church, and the violent oppression of women and of nonelite men. Not without cause, intellectuals and the uneducated alike believed that the end of the world was looming.

Anabaptist groups exemplify communities that provided an alternative vision to such a life on earth, albeit often couched in the discourse of apocalyptic vision, a vision that today may seem repulsive in its wrath wreaked upon the earth. Anabaptists, like their counterparts in the monastic orders, embraced ascetic practices as a way of life. Subject to severe persecution resulting in widespread slaughter, they nevertheless survived. Why were they severely persecuted?

"Anabaptist" refers to those communities that rejected infant baptism, in favor of adult baptism. Such lay groups appeared throughout the Middle Ages (for example, the Albigensians or Cathars and the Waldensians), but they particularly flourished during the Protestant Reformation of the sixteenth century. Considered heretical by Protestants and Catholics alike, the earliest ones of that century emerged in Zurich, Switzerland, in response to religious reforms made by Huldrych Zwingli. The movement, largely populated by peasants, took many different forms ranging from libertine to anti-trinitarian in doctrine and practice. Most groups, however, formed communities that sought to live quite literally by the Sermon on the Mount (for example, Hutterites, Mennonites, and the Amish). For example, many of them were opposed to violence based on their interpretation of turning the other cheek. While later groups tended toward spirit possession (Quakers and Shakers, for example), sixteenth-century communities differed from one another on issues ranging from property ownership to the Incarnation, from holding multiple wives in common to celibacy. The early Mennonites, the Amish, the Brethren, and the later Quakers, nevertheless, stood in agreement on refusal to take oaths, the practice of nonviolence, the separation of church and state, and the freedom of conscience, the bedrock of religious freedom.

Driven by persecution to live separately from the dominant culture, Anabaptists tended to become materially self-sufficient, frugal communities. They also privileged meeting the needs of all members over supplying the wants of some. Anabaptists on the whole rejected the accumulation of goods or wealth. In regard to self-government they held democratically to a priesthood of all believers, though initially (and in some cases continuing into today) men were privileged over women in respect to communal decision-making power. Lastly, they insisted that individual righteousness (right practice) was necessary to salvation, not faith alone as Lutherans and Reformed Protestants argued. Though Protestants and Catholics throughout western Europe made every effort to eradicate them, they have continued to survive, the Mennonites and Quakers in particular, characterized by strong commitments to social outreach to address issues of poverty, injustice, and environmental abuse. This outreach has, over time, relocated these communities more within the dominant culture though in critical relation to it.

Most importantly, just as the Protestant work ethic became a component essential to the success of secular capitalism, so too, Anabaptist values of religious freedom have come to constitute one of the fundamental assumptions of secular democratic freedom in the United States today. The records left to us from the Anabaptists of the sixteenth century tell us little of joy; on the whole they are records of martyrdom at the hands of Catholics and Protestants alike. For an example of happiness produced by joy, we must turn to the present-day Sisters of St. Joseph.

The Sisters of St. Joseph of Carondelet

The Sisters of St. Joseph originated in Le Puy, France, in 1650, only a few generations after the emergence of the Anabaptist Movement. Founded by a small number of women with few material resources (only two of them brought any financial dowry with them) under the auspices of Jesuit Jean Paul Medaille, the Sisters were granted status as an apostolic order as opposed to a monastic order. The apostolic communities, a response by the Catholic Church to rising Protestantism and Anabaptist radicalism, lived out their commitments to poverty, chastity, and obedience in service of the people, rather than withdraw from them, dedicated only to prayer, as the monastic orders did. Thus, apostolic orders differed from the monastic orders in that they did not require a common, daily, rigorous liturgical life. The Sisters' initial purposes were to educate and to care for the sick, their ministry directed especially but not exclusively at women. One of the earliest tasks taken on by the Sisters of St. Joseph of Le Puy was to provide alternative means for economic self-support to local prostitutes by teaching them to tat lace, a lace that came to be known uniquely as "le Puy lace." The Sisters themselves, rather than donning habits, wore the widows' garb of laywomen. Nothing of this tells me that they lived an ascetic life.

In 1836, six Sisters of St. Joseph of Le Puy came to the United States from Lyon to Carondelet, Missouri, and settled in the small, poverty stricken village outside St. Louis. One of their first projects in Missouri was to build a school for the deaf. Later, in 1851 four sisters traveled up the Mississippi Territory to build a school for the children of the new settlers of what was to become Minnesota. A year and a half later the Sisters converted the school into a hospital (Minnesota's first) to care for victims of cholera.

Since the arrival of the Sisters of St. Joseph in the United States, other communities have been established throughout the country. While they share overall values and commitments to love and serve God and neighbor, the individual communities each have the power to determine their own immediate projects in response to the specific needs of the locality. The community I studied directly and on which I will focus here is the St. Paul, Minnesota community where I live. What follows is based on interviews with various members. I am especially grateful to Sister Meg Gillespie, who not only gave me extensive interviews and additional textual and visual resources, but also read this section of my essay carefully and made wonderful suggestions for revisions that strengthened my analysis. (Any errors are, however, mine alone.)

Located in an area called Highland Village, the St. Paul community is significant for this discussion because of the joy or happiness characteristic of the Sisters as they daily pursue sustainable living in a context of social justice. Even as they have sought through a number of projects to leave as small a carbon footprint as possible, they have also worked locally on social justice issues ranging from immigration to involving local hotels in the fight against the sex trafficking of children and adults. The community is particularly known for its openness and willingness to work ecumenically across Christian traditions and with Jews and Muslims.

In 2005, the Sisters found that they needed to improve and update their retirement facilities. After much study, research, and thought they realized that the senior demographic was growing not only among the general population throughout the country, but also particularly in the immediate area. In keeping with their mission "to serve the dear neighbor," they decided to expand the retirement center to serve the broader community. Thus began a long process of thinking through how and where to build such a space.

A steering committee of Sisters worked with professionals and agencies in the health-care field to move to an innovative concept of care based on a person-centered medical model. They hoped for a home that would be comfortable, one that could tailor meals and activities to individual needs, rather than a predetermined, one-size-fits-all schedule. They planned a homey environment, stimulating while peaceful. Most importantly, the residence would be built to be sustainable, in keeping with an emphasis on the sacredness of the universe and concern for the survival of the earth's life resources.

To accomplish these goals, the Sisters needed a partner in the health-care field so that planning was comprehensive. Flexibility and the ability to take risks were needed for the Sisters and their ally. After a long, thorough search procedure, the Sisters established a 50–50 relationship with Presbyterian Homes and Services. The mission, vision, and values of each organization complemented the other well.

One cannot help but be struck by the sheer effort involved in such a process. The research necessary is by itself daunting. It requires new knowledge, ranging from environmental engineering to architecture, from the different needs associated with aging to interior design, from the more specific needs of the local neighborhood to green landscaping.

At least as significant is the imagination required. The sisters wisely traveled to various parts of the country to study how others had implemented person-centered care. At the same time, they had to design innovative ways to address the uniqueness of what they sought to accomplish. They also had to bring to bear all their analytical skills to interview and decide upon the skills and abilities of specialists with whom they would ally themselves. There was always the issue of budget as well. The sheer amount of time involved boggles the mind. Consider further that this time was spent while keeping up with other projects as well. What an undertaking.

Conclusion

The original Anabaptists have transformed over time in a number of different directions, more and less intertwined with the dominant culture. The Amish seek to sustain their separate existence as a community, sadly with less and less success. By contrast, the ongoing efforts made by Mennonites and Quakers toward planetary repair in the context of social justice allow them to live in the world but not of it. These efforts of engagement with the world seem less defensive than the separatism of the Amish, more in keeping with the initial impetus to live according to the Gospels. In all three cases, however, their practice of religious freedom, unhampered by the civil state, continues as a legacy that has extended well beyond their own initial boundaries, a cherished ideal if not always a reality.

The Sisters of St. Joseph got their start squarely in the midst of a culture whose immediate needs they sought to address from the bottom up. The support they received from the Church has allowed them a security not accorded the Anabaptists who nevertheless survived attempted genocide. Al the same, just as the Anabaptists have bestowed a treasured freedom on us, so the good sisters give us a priceless gift as well.

The Sisters' most striking characteristic and greatest gift to me today is their enduring attitude of hope, relative serenity, and joy. These traits that empower them to live sustainably and to work tirelessly on behalf of others challenge easy reduction of ascetic practices to sadomasochistic self-torment, sustained dourness, and the rejection of creation in its beauty. Such an enduring habit of heart and work also challenges retreat from this world, hopelessness, and despair. Practices of self-denial in favor of a simpler life directed toward others train Sisters of St. Joseph of Carondelet to a perspective that I would call critical joy. In one interview I asked Sister Meg how the community could be so hopeful and tireless in the face of overwhelming catastrophe and the high probability of overall failure. The sister explained how the members of the community draw strength from one another and from working with other groups. She described how deeply they care for the earth and for those who suffer injustice upon it. She pointed out that regardless of failure or success, there was life beyond the planet. She concluded, quite simply, "I think of myself and of all of us as allied with divine creativity, God's creativity."

I have pondered this statement, as well as what she didn't say, ever since. She didn't tell me not to worry, that things weren't as bad as they seem. She didn't suggest that I get a grip and "man up." She didn't deny my description of how awful things are. She didn't need to. Whatever the world may look like at this moment, the Sisters of St. Joseph of Carondelet draw energy from a different reality, one that nevertheless embraces this world in all its tragedy and potential doom. Their ascetic practices of living sustainably in service to others derive their impetus and strength less from denying this world and even less from perfecting it. Quite the contrary, the community turns without the usual assurances of personal afterlife, an unlimited human future, or an eventual utopia on earth, directly to the divine creativity with which they have allied, one that they generously share with each other and the world to which they minister. Through this lens, ascetic practices seem less a sacrifice or duty and more a pleasure and a privilege. By contrast, sustaining the current level of materialism seems to demand far more effort with far less reward.

References

Foucault. Michel. 1990. *The History of Sexuality: Introduction*. Vol. 1. Translated by Robert Hurley. New York: Vintage Books.

Hillerbrand, Hans J. ed. 2009. *The Protestant Reformation: Revised Edition*. New York: Harper Perennial.

Scarry, Elaine. 1985. *The Body in Pain: The Making and Unmaking of the World*. New York: Oxford University Press.

Valantasis, Richard, et al., eds. 2006. *The Subjective Eye: Essays in Culture, Religion, and Gender in Honor of Margaret Miles*. Eugene, OR: Pickwick.

Wimbush, Vincent L. and Richard Valantasis, eds. 1998. *Asceticism*. New York: Oxford University Press.

CHAPTER 6

"Dead in the Water.... Again": Life, Liberty, and the Pursuit of Happiness in the Twenty-First Century

Teresa Delgado

On October 21, 2010, CNN premiered the documentary *Black in America: Almighty Debt*, hosted by Soledad O'Brien, which, at the time, was CNN's latest installment in a series of news documentaries about African Americans in the United States. Featured in the 90-minute program was Rev. Dr. DeForest B. Soaries Jr., Senior Pastor of the First Baptist Church of Lincoln Gardens in Somerset, New Jersey. In addition to his multiple pastoral duties, the documentary highlighted Rev. Soaries's philosophy of financial autonomy that he advocates for his 7,000-member congregation. His "dfree™" strategy teaches people how to achieve financial independence, which means "living without debt, deficits and delinquencies." When O'Brien asked Rev. Soaries which was the greater obstacle for African Americans, racism or debt, he responded without hesitation, "Debt is the new slavery...paying last month's bills with next month's income is a kind of indentured servitude. It is financial bondage."

I have to admit that I held back tears for the entire time I watched this program because I also witnessed the reaction of my spouse of 23 years, who had been unemployed since March of 2009. While the documentary showcased the lives of a couple on the verge of losing their home, a young man contemplating how to pay for college, and a 50-something man trying to reinvent his career after hundreds of interviews and rejections, I wondered how he could stomach the reality that we were living all three of these scenarios at once. When I asked him what he was thinking during a commercial break, he responded, "I don't think I can hold my breath under water for much longer. Something's gotta give."

Under water. That is the term used to describe mortgages exceeding the value of a home, a term with which our household is all too familiar as we struggle to negotiate a loan modification to keep a roof over our four children. It is a term used to illustrate the mounting debt that has occurred for many as a result of a loss of income while trying to maintain the necessities of food, clothing, and shelter. It is even a term referenced in the financial crisis that circled the globe in the latter months of 2008, a financial "tsunami" that swept over every sector of the global economy, most directly the financial services industry that was both largely to blame and of which my spouse was a direct victim.

Our situation and the ones highlighted in the CNN documentary are not unique or isolated, unfortunately. While 24-hour news channels report an improved economic outlook since 2009, the unemployment numbers tell quite a different story, even more differentiated by race and ethnicity. According to the most recent Department of Labor Statistics report (www.bls.gov), the unemployment rate for African Americans was 14.3 percent in October of 2012, which isn't the highest reported unemployment rate since the financial crisis began but still higher than the national average. This is compared to the unemployment rate of 10.3 percent for Latinos/as, which does not capture the millions of undocumented workers in the United States who have been devastated by the financial crisis. By contrast, the unemployment rate for white Americans was 7.0 percent, with the national unemployment rate at 7.9 percent in October 2012.

I couldn't help but think of the way Rev. Soaries identified the financial situation in which so many Americans find themselves—as the "new slavery"—in relation to the way in which African Americans were herded into the "old slavery." At the height of the transatlantic slave trade, millions of Africans were taken from the continent against their will, shackled, and packed onto ships en route to the Americas to constitute an enslaved labor force for a growing colonial economy. In that process where, according Emory University's database on the slave trade, over 12.5 million Africans left the shores of their continent, an average of 14 percent died on board the slave ship prior to reaching its destination (www.slavevoyages.org). Accounts of slave voyages document the practice of throwing diseased and dead bodies overboard, so that the remains of almost 2 million Africans mark a trail between Africa and the Americas. Under water.

The profound implications of both the old slavery and the new will continue to impact our country for generations. It took hundreds of years to overturn the most blatant discriminatory laws even after the old slavery was abolished, with much work still left undone. And it will take many years to undo the devastating effect of this financial crisis on the Black community, as the CNN documentary emphasized, as well as on so many other communities already on the verge of poverty. Yet, what struck me the most in relation to my own family experience is the fact that my spouse was born and raised in the Congo, the source of so many slaves transported to the Americas by the Spaniards and Portuguese. While his own immediate ancestors seemed to have escaped the direct consequence of the old slavery, his own immediate descendants—our four children—will certainly endure the direct consequences of the new. The question remains: How do we save our children from dying under water yet again?

I am stumped by that question, practically and theologically. Its enormity gives me pause throughout the day and wakes me from sleep at night. When my own spouse contemplates whether it would benefit our children's future more if he were dead so that we could collect his life insurance policy to relieve our financial burden, I wonder how different is this from throwing a body overboard? How can we make ethical choices when one must choose between two desperate options, both of which feel like drowning?

The words of the Declaration of Independence are all too familiar— "We hold these truths to be self-evident, that all men are created equal, that they are endowed by their Creator with certain unalienable Rights that among these are Life, Liberty and the pursuit of Happiness"—and yet are so far from the experience of all those under the bondage of the new slavery of unemployment/underemployment and financial ruin. The inalienable right to life referenced here entails both the ability to survive and to thrive, embracing both the sanctity of life and the quality of life. The inalienable right to liberty entails the right to be free from that which enslaves or binds one's life, as well as the right to be free for a creative contribution to life. The inalienable right to the pursuit of happiness entails the ability to work toward one's positive aspirations and goals, inclusive of one's family and community. While these affirmations were made to establish a new, independent political system in the United States of America in 1776, we cannot divorce our current economic system from the political entity that has evolved since. When our financial system is so deeply intertwined with our political structure, we must ask ourselves how each serves, enhances, or diminishes the other. The most recent Occupy Wall Street demonstrations suggest that a significant number of our citizens believe that our political and financial systems are in collusion with each other to the benefit of an elite few, which does not include, among others, the vast majority of people of color in this country.

The collusion of the elite 1 percent to further their own interest is at the core of the message resounding from those who claim to be the 99 percent of the US population, struggling for a better life, genuine liberty, and the pursuit of greater happiness. Evidenced by the sweeping resonance of this message taking hold in many other cities across the country—from Boston and Chicago to Denver and Oakland—many people beyond the African American community are feeling as if they are gasping for air under the waters of an economic tidal wave. The gridlock among our political leaders in Washington who have failed to offer meaningful solutions to this crisis seems to indicate that either they do not personally feel the effect of the financial tsunami, or they do not care about the plight of so many of their constituents because their allegiances are elsewhere. In either case, the persistence of this crisis makes it more challenging for the vast majority of our citizens to envision life, liberty, and the pursuit of happiness in their own lifetime. Neither the leaders in Washington nor those on Wall Street are helping to answer the question of how we can save our children from dying under water yet again.

But I'm not a politician, or an economist. I do not know the language of these professions to assert a clear political or economic remedy. However, as a Christian theologian who has devoted her professional life to discerning the ways in which the Gospel message can be interpreted as life-giving, liberating, good news for our time, my obligation is to make explicit the values that should guide us as a society and a nation, the values that must guide our economy and all societal institutions. In this sense, our national aspirations of independence reflected in the quoted selection of our Declaration and the Gospel message of love and justice share a common purpose and, in doing so, potentially wield a fierce indictment against the financial structure of our country that severely undermines both.

In the past, the Gospel of life, liberty, and happiness was able to penetrate the deepest and most entrenched slave experience such that the Christian message held onto by the slave population was quite different from that professed by Christian slave holders. The Gospel message of hope and salvation sustained African Americans during their enslavement, and provided a catalyst for the resistance movements that these groups organized. The Gospel message provided an underpinning to the Civil Rights Movement, grounded in the Christian theology of liberation for the poor, and appropriated by disenfranchised Black folk. We can lift up many other occasions in our nation's history—from the Catholic Worker Movement of Dorothy Day to the United Farm Worker Movement led by Cesar Chavez and Delores Huerta to the Sanctuary Movement in the 1980's—where the prophetic message of the Gospel compelled the country to live up to its self-evident truth. In this moment of crisis for our entire country, the Gospel message of life, liberty, and happiness has the potential to do the same. In fact, Christian theologians have a responsibility to lift up the voices of those who hunger and thirst for justice in these devastating economic times; and if we do not, we are no different than those who continue to perpetuate the laws, regulations, and policies that keep every unemployed person of every race and ethnicity, under water.

To be sure, there are voices from within the Christian churches that propose a distinct message of financial prosperity in the name of Jesus. Some, like Joel Osteen (www.joelosteen.com) and Creflo Dollar, have built multimillion-dollar enterprises with mega-church congregations around the message of the Prosperity Gospel. I can understand how that message strikes a chord among people who have been impoverished for so long, who have struggled, suffered, and died on the multiple crosses of poverty, hunger, unemployment, especially in a country that claims to be the land of opportunity, wealth, and prosperity. But if the Christian understanding of the cross teaches us anything, it should remind us that Jesus's death by crucifixion was not of his own doing, but suffered at the hands of a political system that saw him as a threat to the authority of the state. Jesus's suffering and death on the cross point back to an unjust Roman empire that nailed him there. In our own time, any suffering and death should compel us to lift a mirror to the societal forces that turn a blind eye and perpetuate injustice. And this includes the suffering and death that is occurring in so many communities as a result of the current financial crisis.

While advocating personal responsibility in personal financial matters, proponents of the Prosperity Gospel fail to acknowledge the systemic injustices that remain in place—predatory financial practices, underemployment of people of color, the lack of living wage legislation—even as few are reaping the blessings of abundance and many are not. From the perspective of the Prosperity Gospel, the difference between those who are "blessed" by abundance and those who aren't is more often attributed to the individual motivation and perseverance of the former, rather than a wider economic structure that promotes their particular prosperity over and above the common good and prosperity of all.

If we listen to the words of Jesus, it is impossible to embrace the unbridled, unregulated activity of capitalist market economy while professing the Gospel message in the same breath. Recent history has demonstrated that policies that concentrate resources to the so-called creators of wealth (in the hope that their prosperity will "trickle down" to the rest) do not serve the best interests of the common good. Likewise, it is impossible to embrace a Prosperity Gospel message of individual blessing and abundance when so many people in this country, like my husband, have persevered with determination within an economic system that will not open the door for them, much less give them an opportunity to prosper. Jesus's words in the Gospel of Matthew describe a "beatific vision" for those who would abide by the will of God by caring for the "least of these" and receive blessings in abundance (Matthew 5: 1–12 NRSV):

> Blessed are the poor in spirit: for theirs is the kingdom of heaven.
> Blessed are the meek: for they shall possess the land.
> Blessed are they who mourn: for they shall be comforted.
> Blessed are they that hunger and thirst after justice: for they shall have their fill.

It seems fitting to consider these "beatitudes" in relation to life, liberty, and the pursuit of happiness since the word itself reflects its Latin root, *beatitudo*, or perfect happiness. Within the Christian tradition, a life of perfect happiness is initiated within community and sacramentalized with water in the Christian rite of baptism. Baptism, shared among every Christian denomination, is a ritual of being immersed under water, and being drawn out of the water by a welcoming community of love and acceptance into new life in Christ. Some believe it to be a true "regeneration" of life through water and the Holy Spirit; others see it as "resuscitation," or reviving of those who would otherwise be dead. Baptism is also understood as a cleansing of sin, a washing away of past transgression into a new way of being. Baptism, then, is a sacrament of hope for new life, profound liberty, and the pursuit of perfect happiness. I can say this with all certainty: my spouse, and the millions of others in this country who are suffering and dying under water, so desperately yearn for a sign of baptismal hope by a loving community ready to draw them up from under the water, back into the land of living.

With that in mind, I would propose the following sermon "from the depths," in the spirit of its original spoken on a mount. While in no way claiming to be authoritative or even divinely inspired, I offer the following expressions of *beatitudo* to give voice to the cries, unheard from under the water, speaking truth to the powers of our day and reminding them of their obligation to live up to the founding aspirations of our country, the truths that we hold as self-evident, giving all the opportunity for a dignified life, authentic liberty, and the pursuit of shared happiness:

> Blessed are the unemployed, for they shall know their lives are precious, not the bottom third in the eyes of God.
>
> Blessed are those who offer understanding, compassion, and a helping hand, for they shall not be forgotten for contributing to the fullness of others' lives.
>
> Blessed are those who refuse to look upon the unemployed as the lepers of society, for they shall be called life-giving friends.
>
> Blessed are those who open doors of opportunity when all others have been shut, for they shall give new life to the rejected and will not be disappointed.
>
> Blessed are those who recognize that the people who created this crisis are still calling the shots on Wall Street and Washington, for they shall inspire true liberty.
>
> Blessed are those who believe that the unemployed want to work, for they shall make a way for the mutual pursuit of happiness.
>
> Blessed are those who understand the anguish and pain, for their kindness shall generate joy and happiness.
>
> Blessed are those who post job listings for real jobs, not ones that have already been filled from the inside, for they shall be called authentic agents of liberty.
>
> Blessed are those who evaluate a person based on qualifications, rather than on credit scores, for they shall be called just.
>
> Blessed are those who fight to keep a roof over a family, who work against foreclosure and homelessness, for they shall give the children new life.
>
> Blessed are those who allow time to reestablish firm footing to pay past-due taxes, for even the tax collectors shall have a place in the kingdom of heaven.
>
> Blessed are those who accept the "overqualified," so they can get back to work again, for they shall find happiness through great productivity.

Blessed are those who provide the skills to obtain a financial life that
is free from debt, deficits, and delinquencies, for they shall promote
true liberty and save the global economy.

Blessed are those who sell useful and necessary financial products
rather than toxic ones, for they shall be known as proper stewards of
a happy life.

Blessed are those who believe in our right to life, liberty, and the
pursuit of happiness, for the long-term, for they shall establish a
legacy.

Blessed are those who continue to hope beyond hope, for they shall be
called architects of a free and joyful life.

Blessed are those who hold on to a dream of living in a land that lives
up to the ideals upon which it was founded, for they shall be called
patriotic.

Blessed are the children who forgive their parents for misguided
financial decisions, for they shall learn the meaning of true
happiness.

Blessed are those who truly believe "this too shall pass," for they shall
see God.

As the Gospel message spoke a prophetic word and invoked prophetic action to realign unjust societal relationships in our country's
past, it has the power to do the same in this present moment. Those
who believe in the truths affirmed in our Declaration of Independence
and professed in Jesus's Beatitudes must hold our political and financial leaders accountable to defend the unalienable rights with which we
have been endowed by our Creator, rights that cannot be undermined
by policies and practices that make these rights accessible only to the
elite few. I am inspired by the work of organizations such as *Interfaith
Worker Justice* (www.iwj.org), *The Poverty Initiative* (www.povertyinitia-
tive.org), and *The Micah Institute* (www.nyts.edu/the-micah-institute),
which, in the prophetic tradition so poignantly articulated by Rabbi
Abraham Joshua Heschel, are "saying NO to ... society, condemning its
habits and assumptions, its complacency, waywardness ... [and] man's
false sense of sovereignty, to his abuse of freedom, to his aggressive,
sprawling pride" (Heschel 1962, xxix). Out of a profound understanding that one's faith tradition requires action in the community, they
are holding our leaders accountable because they are part of that same
community, equally responsible to and for the common good.

Just as the church invites members into a new life through the sacrament of baptism, bringing us out from under the water into renewed
being where our life, liberty, and happiness are never separated from

that of our beloved community, we must now create a circle of love and care to bring those out from under the water of financial despair into a new life of promise. Within the halls of Congress, to the boardrooms of Wall Street, and everywhere in between, all who claim to live under the banner of our Declaration of Independence must reach down into the murkiest of waters, where death seems inevitable, to draw up those who are drowning back to life, into renewed liberty, and a hopeful promise for happiness. This is how we can, and must, save our children from dying under the water yet again.

References

Dollar, Creflo A. Jr. 1999. *Total Life Prosperity: 14 Practical Steps to Receiving God's Full Blessing.* Nashville, TN: Thomas Nelson.

Gutierrez, Gustavo. 1990. *The Truth Shall Make You Free: Confrontations.* Maryknoll, NY: Orbis Books.

Heschel, Rabbi Abraham Joshua. 1962. *The Prophets.* Vol. 1. New York: Harper Torch Books.

Manson, Jamie L. 2011. "Crucifixion Helps Make Meaning of Pain in Church, World." *National Catholic Reporter Online.* April 20.

Osteen, Joel. 2010. *It's Your Time: Activate Your Faith, Achieve Your Dreams and Increase in God's Favor.* New York: Free Press / Simon and Schuster.

Recinos, Harold J. 2006. *Good News from the Barrio: Prophetic Witness for the Church.* Louisville, KY: Westminster John Knox Press.

Soaries, Rev. Dr. DeForest B. Jr. 2011. *dfree™ Breaking Free from Financial Slavery.* Grand Rapids, MI: Zondervan.

The Trans-Atlantic Slave Trade Database. 2009. Sponsored by Emory University. Available at www.slavevoyages.org.

US Bureau of Labor Statistics. Available at www.bls.gov.

CHAPTER 7

Welcome to the Great American Middle Class: From the American Dream to Deep Solidarity

Joerg Rieger

For a long time, the American middle class assumed that it was living the American Dream. A certain standard of personal wealth, job security, and social benefits were taken for granted. Motivated by religious injunctions to "love your neighbor as yourself" and a feeling of *noblesse oblige*, people were willing to "give back" to the community. Volunteer spirit is higher in the United States than in many other countries. Charity is a common value and is practiced in particular by members of churches and other religious organizations. Soup kitchens for the hungry, clothes closets for the needy, meals on wheels for the elderly, and work projects that help fix up dilapidated neighborhoods are among the many examples. Those even more determined to give back to the community have typically engaged in advocacy projects. Such advocacy projects include support of human rights projects both at home and abroad, dealing with matters that range from the abandonment of the death penalty to fair trade, and the eradication of various forms of racism.

Now, members of the middle class are increasingly experiencing in their own lives the pressures that have crushed those whom they sought to help. The so-called Great Recession that began at the end of 2007 has affected the middle class unlike any recession since the Great Depression. Unlike in other recessions, things are not projected to improve quickly for most people, as half of the jobs that were lost are not expected to come back. At present according to shadowstats.com, as much as 23 percent of the US population is unemployed or under-employed. Layoffs continue and are affecting the middle class more and more, while the new jobs that are being created offer less money, fewer benefits, and less security. The future of savings and retirement plans, staples of middle-class life that used to guarantee stability and peace of mind, is uncertain after these plans took major hits.

Even professionals who once located themselves in the upper echelons of the middle class are experiencing pressures. In the academy, for instance, the economic rules of "mean and lean production" are increasingly applied, and at present there is a push for "outcomes evaluations," which measure not the quality of work that is produced but a list of rather superficial indicators. Religious communities like churches offer little relief, as they are more than ever driven by membership rolls and budgets, affecting the lives of religious professionals and members alike.

In this context, which is marked by what I have called the "logic of downturn" (Rieger 2009), our perspectives on life, liberty, and the pursuit of happiness change. At first this change may be hardly noticeable, but things may never be the same. That our visions of life, liberty, and happiness can be changed in ways that are more promising for the flourishing of human life is my hope, to which I will come back at the end.

The American Dream and the American Volunteer Spirit

One of the casualties of our current impasse may well be the American Dream itself, which holds that anyone can make it in this great country. Unfortunately, this dream has been merely a fantasy for most Americans. Surprisingly, social mobility in the United States is lower than in many of our peer countries (Hertz 2006). Still, many Americans were raised to believe that this dream was within reach, if not for them, then at least for their children. Such hopes are fading fast not only because the economic crisis lingers everywhere, except at the very top, but also because the foundations of middle-class wealth are vanishing with the disappearance of good jobs and the ongoing loss of housing values in most parts of the country.

Just as the American Dream undergoes a reality check, so too might the American volunteer spirit. According to the federal Corporation for National and Community Service (CNCS), a government institution, volunteer spirit has not decreased but risen between 2008 and 2009.

1.6 million more Americans volunteered in 2009 than in 2008, when volunteering had taken a dip, which makes it the largest increase since 2003. While we are not informed about what happened after 2009, what drives this upsurge, and whether it is sustainable, are questions yet to be answered. One reason for the increase is that many people at this time cannot afford not to volunteer. In a tightening job market, volunteering is a proven way to strengthen a resume, as it adds distinction and maintains the middle-class spirit. For aspiring college students, volunteer work functions in similar ways.

This sort of volunteering is no longer as voluntary as it once was. It has become part of the expectations of corporate America, which spruces up its image by encouraging volunteer projects and, for this purpose, has even redirected some of the funds that once went to internal social events, to volunteer projects. In this climate, the volunteer organizations that benefit the most are the ones that have name recognition, while others dwindle. The causes seen as more urgent because they deal with basic needs of food, shelter, and transportation have greater clout than the ones that deal with the arts, the environment, and long-term health issues (Shaw 2009). Volunteering in terms of advocacy does not even show up on these lists.

Despite these pragmatic concerns that drive the volunteer spirit, volunteering and the American Dream remain connected. Belief in the American Dream supports a volunteer spirit, and volunteering supports the American Dream. Religious communities in the United States frequently support both. But what will happen to the volunteer spirit as the American Dream changes shape? And what will happen as people are less and less able to give back because they do not have the means or the time to serve the community? Even the unemployed are busier than ever before, as looking for a job has become a full-time occupation, with job seminars, continuing education, applications, and interviews that come in many different shapes and forms.

Solidarity and Advocacy

Volunteering to help others is often seen as a form of solidarity. Nevertheless, this solidarity harbors some problems. When some students and faculty of Perkins School of Theology began volunteering with a project that fixed up houses in a poor West Dallas neighborhood, we emphasized mutuality, and the fact that we were building two-way street relationships where both sides learn. All that some participants seemed to learn, however, was how fortunate they were compared to their destitute neighbors. Similar results happened on church mission trips all the time. Many Christian youth groups in Texas came back from Mexico, for instance, celebrating the economic well-being of their families and their large refrigerators rather than reflecting on the struggles they witnessed. This sort of solidarity is built on feelings of *noblesse oblige*, coupled with the American Dream that anyone can make it, feelings that are frequently found in middle-class religious communities.

Volunteering in advocacy projects introduces a different attitude because the goal is not merely to address immediate needs of other people but also the problems that cause these needs. Solidarity for those who practice advocacy, most of them members of the middle class, is not limited to supplying aid but extends to supporting and strengthening people in their efforts to overcome what causes the problem. It is one thing to supply the unemployed with food, shelter, and transportation, and it is quite another to speak up on their behalf, for example to campaign for a stop in unemployment benefits and the creation of decent jobs. It is one thing to build cinder block homes in Mexico and it is quite another to protest the working conditions in the *maquiladoras*, which pay their workers so poorly that they are not able to afford decent housing. Here, solidarity includes an understanding of how policies like the North American Free Trade Agreement are used against workers, and efforts to bring these problems before the public and lawmakers who can do something about them. Religious communities have lent support to some of these advocacy projects, although it is my impression that they are less fashionable now with religious people than they were ten or twenty years ago. Taking a stand and advocating for justice is increasingly branded as creating conflict.

Volunteers who engage in advocacy understand that it is not enough to ameliorate the symptoms of a problem, and that little will change until we go to the bottom of it and address the underlying conflict that is mostly covered up. From this vantage point, questions arise as to whether everyone has equal access to the American Dream. Since many volunteers who engage in advocacy continue to believe in the American Dream, they seek to level the playing field so that all will have a chance to thrive. In the United States, leveling the playing field involves particular programs like Head-Start programs in schools that serve underprivileged neighborhoods, after-school tutoring for children from families with fewer resources, and affirmative action programs that give preference to those who would otherwise be disadvantaged. Several of these programs are volunteer-driven, including community organizing efforts, where neighborhoods organize to petition for support from local governments for schools and other public projects like basketball courts. Religious communities are sometimes involved in these projects, through organizations like the Industrial Areas Foundation and the Gamaliel Foundation. The concern of these organizations is advocacy for justice and stronger communities rather than charity.

Not surprisingly, these forms of volunteer work receive less support from corporate America than volunteer projects that engage in charity. Nevertheless, corporate America and politicians support some programs when they apply pressure and manage to organize the masses. Community organizing programs consistently find support from officials when they rally thousands of people in support of concrete projects like school lunches or playgrounds. Corporate sponsors for such projects can also be found, as playgrounds or gyms might be named for a corporation or a philanthropist. Advocacy for fair trade with farmers in poorer countries has also been successful, as fair-trade coffee, for instance, is now sold by national chains and groceries, right alongside coffee produced by corporations. This sort of advocacy can still be done in the name of a fairly unreconstructed American Dream, according to which everybody continues to have an opportunity to make it.

The "Dream Act" program, a bipartisan congressional bill, which supports a conditional path to citizenship for children of undocumented immigrants that meet stringent requirements, prominently announces its faith in the American Dream. According to the bill's website, the claim is that these youth should "get the opportunity to test their dreams and live their American story" just like everyone else. Surely, this solidarity has its value, as many people's lives are improved or even empowered. This is especially important in the current climate when charity has become the dominant model, with its often-patronizing flavor that hardly ever questions the status quo and thus supports it by default.

While some advocacy for justice is thus supported, advocacy encounters resistance when more straightforward accounts of the underlying problems are given. Compare for example community organizing, which helps communities get a slice of the American pie, and labor organizing, which addresses how this pie is baked and why the slices of some increase in size while the slices of all others continue to be trimmed back. Corporate support for these latter positions is hard to imagine, as labor organizing questions the role of the corporations and who benefits from current economic arrangements.

Deep Solidarity: The Hurdles

These two options, charity and advocacy, are commonly understood as the only ones, especially for members of the American middle class. Yet there is one more form of solidarity that needs to be addressed. The conditions appear to be right for this form of solidarity, which I am calling deep solidarity (Rieger and Kwok 2012), to rise again. Deep solidarity has existed at various times and in various ways and forms in the past, often among the lower and working classes. Although it has never completely disappeared, in the context of the current options it looks new, simply because it has been pushed underground and remained there for a long time. Shortly after I wrote these lines, the Occupy Movement popularized the notion that "we are the ninety-nine percent," which is another manifestation of what I am talking about. Now the challenge is to create a deeper understanding of what this means.

Deep solidarity begins with the simple realization that many of us are in the same boat—many more of us than we ever imagined. Deep solidarity is not a decision of the will to help the less fortunate or to advocate for them. Instead, deep solidarity presupposes an understanding that there is no neutral position and no safe middle ground, which is one of the fundamental illusions of the middle class. Thus, deep solidarity means that taking sides is now not simply an option for a few committed people but a requirement for all. Not taking sides in a situation of grave power imbalances, similar to the present US situation, means supporting the side of the powers that be.

The insight that there is no safe middle ground, as interests of the dominant class have taken over more and more of our lives, has deep implications for the American Dream and how we imagine life, liberty, and the pursuit of happiness in this country. American corporate law frames the basic issue: corporations and their leadership are accountable to their stockholders and not to their workers (Rieger 2009, chapter 2). Put as bluntly as possible, the law requires that the well-being of stockholders is to be pursued at the expense of the well-being of the workers, clearly delineating the group that has a right to benefit from the American Dream and whose liberty and happiness deserve to be protected.

This situation creates a class struggle that is waged against the 99 percent, and it is no secret who is waging it and who is winning it. To be sure, even most people who own stocks are not on the winning side, as the vast majority of stock is held by a relatively small number of large investors. In 2006, Warren Buffett, one of the world's top investors and the third-wealthiest person in the world at the time of this writing, noted when asked about class struggle in an interview with *The New York Times*: "There's class warfare, all right. But it's my class, the rich class, that's making war, and we're winning" (Stein 2006). Buffet's surprising confession, repeated in 2011, led him to call for higher taxes for wealthy Americans, a call that was quickly pushed under the rug. If not even one of the wealthiest people in the world can turn history around by himself, deep solidarity may be our last hope.

Class struggle manifests itself in our current economic situation, where the wealthy get wealthier while the unemployment crisis is worsening. To add insult to injury, this crisis is used to pressure those who still hold jobs to give up benefits and hard-earned privileges. The large number of unemployed is used to pressure those who are employed to work harder and more for less. In some factories, workers who are laid off at the end of the week still get to see the new schedules that add the work that they were doing to the work load of their colleagues. Class struggle also manifests itself in labor laws that make it very difficult for workers to organize and to represent their own interests—a human right recognized by the United Nations—thus effectively restricting the liberty of workers in favor of the liberty of the corporation. The Employee Free Choice Act (EFCA), a bill before Congress that would have made it easier for workers to form unions, has been stalled for years. Class struggle, furthermore, manifests itself in cultural networks like religious communities, where wealthy donors (both actual and potential) have more say than other members, including clergy and bishops. Class, therefore, is not just a matter of wealth but also of power.

But if the law requires that the well-being and happiness of stockholders is to be pursued, does that not include large parts of the middle class? Are we not all stockholders now, as even our retirement plans are tied to mutual funds and the stock market? While we are made to believe that there is another deep solidarity among stockholders—without this term being used—the problem is that there is an enormous gap between those who hold some stock and the major stockholders. While in politics we follow the principle "one person, one vote," in economics we follow the principle "one share, one vote." If our political processes are skewed due to campaign financing and maneuvers like districting and redistricting, economic processes may be further skewed. Thus, some economists have argued that the seemingly sound idea of investing retirement funds in the stock market is not so sound after all, as economic power is extremely skewed (Wolman and Colamosca 2003). As we have seen in the recent crisis, the losses accrue at the bottom and top investors keep gaining as small investors go bankrupt.

More examples could be given for why the middle class does not find itself safely in the middle but is increasingly worn thin in a class struggle that is waged from the top. In sum, the situation of the middle class is more precarious than we tend to admit, as more and more people have been unemployed for long periods of time, having used up retirement funds before the beginning of retirement, or lost their houses. In addition, as workload increases while salaries and benefits are further cut, the remaining retirement accounts are less than secure, and Social Security and Medicare are under attack, the future of the middle class looks not very promising. When this is acknowledged, a kind of deep solidarity emerges that actually makes sense. So, what is it that still prevents us from bonding with all those others who are benefiting even less from the way things are at the moment?

First of all, deep solidarity will not gain us brownie points with corporate America and may lead to even greater repercussions. Spearheading a fund drive for a charity is valued differently than spearheading a labor organizing drive. Handing out meals is valued differently than raising questions in public about why so many people do not have access to decent meals in a wealthy country like the United States. Unfortunately, the same value scale that is applied by corporations is also applied by many organizations that are charged with pursuing the public's interest and happiness rather than the stockholders' interest and happiness, including schools, universities, and religious communities.

Second, deep solidarity may initially get us even more in trouble in a troubled world. Organizing workers, whether blue collar or white collar, is difficult today because they have reason to fear repercussions even when they simply commiserate with other workers. Too often, workers who speak up about problems at their workplace are let go and blacklisted for future jobs. Even those who have traditionally considered themselves professionals, like doctors, lawyers, ministers, and academics, can get blacklisted. Organizing unemployed people is even more difficult. Many of them have valuable first-hand information about how class struggle is waged against working people, but they know that talking about these experiences puts them at a disadvantage in the search for jobs. Also, the many different seminars for job seekers have at least one thing in common: they put the responsibility for unemployment and success squarely in the lap of their clients, who are thus prevented from entering into solidarity (Ehrenreich 2005).

Deep Solidarity: The Potential

Despite all these hurdles, the middle class now has a unique opportunity to move from advocacy to deep solidarity. Such solidarity becomes possible when members of the middle class are beginning to experience their location in the tensions between the ruling class and the working class. Deep solidarity differs from more common notions of solidarity in that it is not another program that seeks to support people who are worse off. Deep solidarity begins with the simple realization that we are in the same boat with other people who have to work for a living— the 99 percent—and farther removed from the ruling class than we thought. Becoming aware of our own plight, we can become more aware of the plight of others as well, which is often worse than our own. While deep solidarity is not supported by corporate America and many public organizations including many mainline churches, it may be exactly what we need. While the various steps from charity to advocacy point in the right direction, deep solidarity pushes us further. As solidarity between working people and the unemployed develops, for instance, the corporations will no longer be able to play off one group against another as easily. The specter of the unemployed can no longer be used to slash salaries and benefits of working people, and working people cannot as easily be cowed into accepting these worsening conditions that are then used to force the unemployed to accept jobs that have even worse working conditions. Deep solidarity is related to the fact that the poor, the working class, and the middle class are more and more welded together by the current climate that benefits the wealthiest, whose wealth keeps increasing as others lose out. In a *Daily Finance* article from March 2011, the number of billionaires is at its highest level ever, and the combined wealth of these billionaires is at an all-time peak. This rising tide neither lifts the boats of the middle class, nor can we expect much trickling down to the common people. Even the recent government bailouts of the banks and financial corporations were directed at the top rather than the bottom.

Yet, deep solidarity is not just related to the experience of common pressure. Deep solidarity produces the kinds of relationships that celebrate the actual work that is done every day by millions of people, and it reinforces the kind of agency that works from the bottom up rather than the top down. The trade unions have understood this point to some degree, as here solidarity is based on a profound sense of the value of work. No matter how ingenious CEOs and their boards may be, nothing would get done without people on the ground who are directly engaged in production of goods and services. The world is not transformed by great ideas alone—an erroneous assumption of middle-class professionals and academics in particular; rather, the world is transformed through creative labor that brings together ideas and labor.

Deep solidarity changes the self-understanding of the middle class. Intellectuals, for instance, are most productive when they are organic intellectuals (Gramsci 1971), that is, when they place themselves in organic relation with working people and when they understand themselves as working people, although they may be given certain privileges by the powers that be. Otherwise, even the most creative intellectuals are condemned to repeating the status quo. This is true in religious communities as well: the endless planning and program committee meetings that clog our schedules maintain the status quo, as they hardly go anywhere without involvement at the grassroots. Here lies the potential of deep solidarity.

From the perspective of deep solidarity, the American Dream can be rewritten and recovered in ways that are truer to what this dream originally represented. Deep solidarity reminds us that this dream is not the dream of the individual whose success is produced at the expense of others, but the dream of a community, which flourishes as all work together for the common good. Deep solidarity reminds us that the US Constitution names as the acting subject not prominent individuals, the president, or the elites, but "We the people."

Deep solidarity, therefore, transforms the notions of life, liberty, and happiness. The lives, liberties, and pursuits of happiness of working people are inextricably related to the ones of the middle class as broadly understood, professionals and small business people included. Here, each of the terms acquires a new depth in meaning: life becomes a collective matter rather than an individual thing that engages the real struggles of our time. Liberty is no longer the liberty of the corporations and the powerful but the liberty of the people, as liberty is better understood as democracy rather than as deregulation of the economy. And happiness, finally, is when everyone can live well and in freedom, not just the elites.

In this changing climate, our concepts of religion, theology, and the church are changing as well, moving away from artificially individualized, privatized, depoliticized, and "deeconomized" models toward communities that resemble more what the prophets and the gospels were talking about. The current religion and labor movements exemplify to some extent what I have in mind, when they promote solidarity with and among working people not as a separate act of social activism but as the core of religion. Celebrating worship in the midst of the tensions of real life—including on the factory floors and picket lines, rather than in pious isolation on the mountaintops—changes our view of religion, ourselves, and ultimately of God, whose deep solidarity with us is manifest in the labors of creation as well as the struggles for liberation that continue through history.

References

Corporation for National and Community Service. Available at http://www.nationalservice.gov/about/volunteering/index.asp.

The DREAM Act. www.dreamact.info. "Forbes: The Richest People in the World 2011." 2011. *Daily Finance*, March 9. Available at http://www.walletpop.com/2011/03/09/forbes-the-richest-people-in-the-world-2011/.

Ehrenreich, Barbara. 2005. *Bait and Switch: The (Futile) Pursuit of the American Dream*. New York: Metropolitan Books.

Gramsci, Antonio. 1971. "The Intellectuals." In *Selections from the Prison Notebooks*. edited and translated by Quintin Hoare and Geoffrey Nowell Smith. 3–23. New York: International Publishers.

Hertz, Tom. 2006. "Understanding Mobility in America." For the Center for American Progress. Available at http://www.americanprogress.org/issues/2006/04/Hertz_MobilityAnalysis.pdf.

Rieger, Joerg. 2009. *No Rising Tide: Theology, Economics, and the Future*. Minneapolis: Fortress Press.

Rieger, Joerg and Kwok, Pui-lan. 2012. *Occupy Religion: Theology of the Multitude*. Religion in the Modern World. Lanham, MD: Rowman and Littlefield Publishers.

Shadow Government Statistics. 2011. "Alternate Unemployment Charts." As of December 2. Available at http://www.shadowstats.com/alternate_data/unemployment-charts.

Shaw, Bob. 2009. "Even in a Recession, Minnesota's Volunteer Spirit Blossoms." *Pioneer Press*, September 19. Available at http://www.tchabitat.org/page.aspx?pid=801.

Stein, Ben. 2006. "In Class Warfare, Guess Which Class is Winning." *The New York Times*, November 26. Available at http://www.nytimes.com/2006/11/26/business/yourmoney/26every.html.

Wolman, William and Anne Colamosca. 2003. *The Great 401 [k] Hoax: Why Financial Security Is at Risk, and What You Can Do about It*. Cambridge, MA: Basic Books.

CHAPTER 8

Political Theology: Reflecting on the Arts of a Liberating Politics

Mark Lewis Taylor

I've written my first poem
I called myself a poet to motivate me to write
Because I knew poets will set us free
In 1998 I was granted parole.
                              —Eddy Zheng "Autobiography@33"

Those of us in theological studies who take seriously our place in public life often undertake "political theology" to join theology with public issues. Just what constitutes political theology today is highly contested (de Vries and Sullivan 2006). I will argue for a political theology *not* because we need an already-constituted guild discipline, Theology (its guild status denoted by a capital "T") to address political problems, making "political theology" a sub-discipline of Theology proper. Instead, I hold that Theology, whatever its subject-matter (God, Christ or church, social justice, existential concerns) is always already political. It has a "politicality," its discourses inscribed in a complex play of public forces of antagonism. Political theology, as I have long proposed, is theological discourse always mindful of its inscription (embeddedness) in antagonisms, generated by assemblages of social constructs: class, empire, race, gender, sexuality, nation. Political theology is also, in Jean-Luc Nancy's sense, an "exscription," a writing-out from bodies suffering these antagonisms, toward an integral liberation. Especially as exscription, political theology, I argue here, is reflection on the arts at work in social movements with liberating impact. In the spirit of Zheng's epigraph above, political theology's discourse arises from sites of enlivening synergy between art and social movement, making liberation thinkable, achievable (Zheng 2007, 40).[1]

Political theology in my approach, then, is a variant of Paul Kahn's definition: "an effort to describe the social imaginary of the political" (Kahn 2011, 26). My notions of "the imaginary," and "the political," though, do not pivot around engagements with German theorist Carl Schmitt, as do Kahn and others in political theology today. From the vantage point of Theology's politicality, I place Theology itself in question, pressing for a radical theological discourse not limited to Theology, certainly not to that of Christian thinkers. Indeed, theological discourse has already migrated toward other spaces—transdisciplinary, intercultural and interreligious, both academic and broadly public (Taylor 2011, 152–158, 222).

I am closer to those theologians, then, who seek critically to locate their work in relation to "the multitude" theorized by Michael Hardt and Antonio Negri (Kwok and Rieger 2012; Crockett and Robbins 2013). I state this with the proviso—and it is a major one—that theorizing the multitude occurs across "the colonial difference" (Mignolo 2011, 16–19), thus resisting Eurocentrism, and highlighting the present class war by neocolonizing and neoliberal powers, which, for the sake of a largely white or honorary "white overclass,"[2] limit and make war against the flesh and flourishing of communities of color among the multitudes of the dispossessed. The "radicality"—the going to the roots—of this political theology is no mere "radical" questioning of God (asserting a "death of God"). Such *may* be necessary. But a deeper radicality grows when political theology's roots drink from the synergy of popular arts and social movements of liberation.

I argue for a political theology, then, as *decolonizing liberation theology,* theoretically shaped over the years, for me, by critical anthropological theory and recent decolonial theory. "Liberation"—better than emancipation, liberty, or even freedom—names the structural, revolutionary futures worked for by decolonizing and deimperializing movements (Hardt and Negri 2009, 331–332). This political theology is indebted not only to well-known "liberation theologies" of recent Latin America, which sometimes presented themselves as "political theology" of liberation (Ellacuría 1973/1976, 95–110), but also to the radical Christianities in the United States and of nearly every continent, especially in the Caribbean, where African, Asian, indigenous, Creole and Mestizo, and also European traditions interplay (Benítez-Rojo, 1996). Such political theology is foreshadowed also by liberating motifs in early Jesus movements and prophetic Judaism, and also in liberating visions, rites, and practices of Muslim, Buddhist, and many traditions. None of these should be romanticized as unsullied sources of solidarity and liberation. But nor should we today forget that the struggle for liberation is ancestral, rooted in a living polycultural past.

Political Theology for Surviving the Times

Especially pertinent to the argument I will make here is the fact that I have found collectively shared art, especially in political and social movements, as veritably life-saving. Even in personal solitude, moving art—creative art that animates social movements against antagonistic structures—is something that keeps me oriented in hope. My own body and the bodies of those dear to me have been mistreated and violated by various constraining modes, ranging from corporate punishment and domestic violence in families, to imprisonment and torture among friends and personal acquaintances.

In print, I have often referenced my work in the US prisons since the years of my training and internship in theological education, particularly in the Virginia State Penitentiary (Taylor 2011, 35–40). In contemporary US mass incarceration, we find a most basic antagonism of flesh, dividing human from human, especially by the onerous divisions of class, gender/sexual, and racial discrimination. The US prisons remain crossroads for the technologies of white racism, hegemonic masculinism, imperialism, and economic exploitation.

My knowledge of the prisons is compounded by years of receiving testimonies of those subjected to torture throughout the Americas—from Chicago's police precinct stations, to immigrant detention centers in the United States, to US military institutions of Central and South America. Add to this the burden one feels belonging to a nation that so freely deploys its military, covert and overt, against so many nations to defend its economic and geopolitical sovereignty (Taylor 2005, 21–23). Much of this history is kept from major textbooks and US public consciousness. Who can maintain a sense of humanity amid a US polis that devises, tolerates, or plans so many massive aerial assaults, while not being burdened, not so much by guilt—though that is often worth owning—but simply by the heaviness of it all, the marked injustice of it? There is little comfort in knowing well that structured violence is not new, with US history featuring Indian slaughter and land theft; brutal centuries of enslaving Africa's descendents; US military interventions (overt and covert) in the Caribbean and Latin America; building "the American century" up from the bombed, burned-over nations of Asia (the Philippines, Japan, the Koreas, Vietnam, Laos, Cambodia), now in Central and West Asia (Afghanistan, Iraq, Iran[3]). Then there's the slow, daily grind of suffering from poverty and curable but untreated diseases, which is the lot of many, a consequence of global financial policies of the once colonizing, still hegemonic global north (Sung 2011; Farmer 2003, 29–50).

These are not simply isolated cases of extreme suffering. To the contrary, daily living in this country—raising our children, drawing cash from an ATM (*if* "we" can), driving our cars—have this structural violence, as their condition of possibility. Thankfully, from this suffering come, too, persistent dreams, practices, and movements that portend change. In nearly all the places of suffering, I long have known the art-force of human creativity under pressure: singing, dancing, weaving, painting, quilting, marching, walking, needlework, and more. I call for a political theology, and politically conscious theologies generally, arising from these fields of agony and hope.

Why Political Theology Now?

Such rethinking of political theology now is made possible by changes in public life and discourse that reshape the way the theological and the political interact. Why are we seeing, for example, avowed atheist thinkers writing positively on the incarnation or the trinity? Why does philosopher Alain Badiou, who "cares nothing for Paul's gospel," write a commentary on St. Paul? Slavoj Žižek writes best-selling books for academics, drawing huge crowds internationally, fusing reflection on Christ's incarnation with Che Guevara, while skewering "political correctness" with a mix of jokes, Hegel, Chesterton, and philosophical rigor. Walter Mignolo criticizes the "theo-logic" of colonialism while endorsing "spiritual" paths toward polycentric, noncapitalist futures. Postcolonial critic Gayatri Chakravorty Spivak dreams of an animist "liberation theology" for our times of corporate exploitation (Taylor 2011, 10).[4] Whether or not these political theorists have a current or nuanced knowledge of theological writings, their own theological turns have prompted theologians to new political theologies (Crockett and Robbins 2012).

Thus, assumptions about the religious beliefs ("the theological") and of power and its social organization ("the political") are being rethought.

In contrast, political and public theologies have all too often presumed, "Well, we have Theology, we know what it is, now we need to address some political or public issues. We have our Christology, for example, now let's spell out its meanings for the public order." That's insufficiently complex for a period in which theology and political theory are engaging one another anew. Indeed, there are theologians who long have crafted political theological discourse anew, questioning theology itself, making liberation an examined ideal (for numerous examples see citations in Taylor 2011, 154n105), but such occurrences as these often are consigned to Theology's margins, finding home mainly in transdisciplinary and public spaces beyond Theology.

Let me cite three of many features, intellectual and cultural, that provoke rethinking of the theological and the political. First, religious and theological beliefs and commitments have reasserted a forceful political presence. In the face of announcements of "a secular age," religion still has vigor, indeed romps through our public orders with new political claws, wielding state power to back religious convictions and/or reinforcing state violence. Liberals, too, have accommodated or been toothless for challenging these fusions of religion with state power (Taylor 2005, 72–86). New thinking on Theology's reasserted political interests, thus, becomes necessary.

Second, this new thinking arises also from a now deeply lodged sense, in academy and public life, of distinctions between being "religious" and being "spiritual." Elites of religious traditions, especially in Theology, have often been dismissive of this, suggesting that those seeking such spiritualities were watering-down the good wine of vintage religious traditions. But ponder a home altar in Brooklyn or in São Paolo, or examine alleged "new age" spiritualities, and one likely finds complex syncretisms of political and theological beliefs that spark fresh viewpoints on theology and politics. Or, just converse with 20-something activists today, with union organizers, various grassroots women's movements, or those the Occupy Movement, hip-hop artists bridging Asian American, Latino/a American, and African American youth struggle (Sharma 2010). Here one finds political interests anew, introducing winsome, political spiritualities.

Third, the range of religious and spiritual resources for political theology is widening. Even for Christian theologians, knowledge of one's own tradition is inadequate for engaging public life. The polycultural interreligiousness of public life means that political theology will rarely be cogent or "public" if done only from one religious tradition. This is a special challenge for US Christian theologians, since, in spite of current interreligious communities, the national milieu remains heavily Christianized.

Guild Theology and "The Transcendent"

Even when some creative thinkers in Christian guild Theology explore new configurations of theological and political life, that guild often remains cloistered, sustaining a Christian privilege vis-à-vis other religious and cultural worlds. Even in liberal guise the guild's intellectual *habitus* often cultivates an "imperio-colonial sense," an interpretive style that accommodates Western Christian nationalisms, especially US imperial projects, remaining silent about racial, economic, gendered, sexual, and racial subordination (Taylor 2011, 49–62). That interpretive style in Theology is usually oriented by references to a divine Other, a transcendent figure beyond or outside world, culture, history.

Some have asked me if I therefore hold Theology "irredeemable," needing to be abandoned. Not necessarily. I remain, myself, in the guild. I learn from many whose thinking struggles for liberation; but in the United States especially, such views as these are usually forced to the margins of Theology, remaining primarily Eurocentric—still predominantly white and often silent, especially when political theologies by scholars of color target white racism (Taylor 2011, 53–62). If Theology fails to adapt to more recent developments, or if it continues to marginalize those who explore the creative discourses of repressed communities, Theology will have little future beyond perpetuating confessionalist ideologies and liberal reform projects for elites. Guild Theology is "irredeemable" only if its commitments to doctrinal language and systems of belief lead it to uncompromising defense of some transcendent Other, and a slighting of popular art forms of a very this-worldly liberating politics

Even when the transcendent is defended as "going immanent," affirming the "immanence *of* the transcendent" or "incarnational transcendence," the world's restless and creative energy is largely marked as derivative, treated mainly as a reflex or "creation" of an external infusion—of "grace," divine power, of an Other's prevenient action. Denoting a transcendent often effects a demoting of the world's own creativity. We might like to think that by means of some immanentalization of the transcendent, our world is "sacralized," "re-enchanted," thus given greater value. It's a beautiful idea, but strategically, in practice, that is not what happens. What happens instead is this: believers look to some Other and slight—often unintentionally, I will grant—the revivifying restlessness of the world itself, thus often giving their support to the chain of sovereign powers in the world. That restlessness, intrinsic to the world, I explore below as "transimmanence."

On a more practical level, I cannot help asking: where were the US churches and their transcendent sovereign Other, which might have been invoked to challenge US global sovereignty, during its international law-breaking invasion and occupation of Iraq in 2003? In that hour, the logics of the transcendent sovereign God were deployed more to bolster the imperial adventuring of US nationalist projects—even in so-called liberal and progressive churches. The theo-logic of the transcendent Other does not have a very good track record in promoting liberating politics of late.

"The Theological" *within* Liberating Social Movements

My own notion of "the theological" has, as its site of arising, the liberating politics of social movements. This is political theology as theology owning its always present "politicality" and then examining it alongside working movements in progress. Such political theology begins with a sense of the agonistic striving of peoples, what I refer to in a kind of shorthand as "the weight of the world." This is not merely the weight we all bear as finite beings—as limitation, anxiety, sickness, death, and so on. No, I mean the weight of those whose finitude is often made more onerous and "weighty" by practices of imposed social suffering, disseminated structural violence we often name gender injustice, racism, class exploitation, and sexual repression/exclusion. These have been interlaced in multiple ways over centuries of intercontinental formations in the "coloniality of power" (Quijano 2000). What a person's or a group's suffering is, its weight, is often determined by where one is amid the colonial matrix of power.

There are many examples today of structural violence or imposed social suffering—I use these terms interchangeably. They include the growing divide between rich and poor in the United States and globally and ways that divide affects peoples' access to care amid sickness and dying (Farmer 2003); the new US racialized regime of imprisonment and social caste, a condition analyzed as "New Jim Crow" (Alexander 2010); this punishment regime's working in tandem with racialized immigrant detention of Latino/a American, Asian American, and Arab American communities (Nguyen 2005, 137–157). Referencing all these is no mere "political correctness." It is to identify spheres of social relations where inequalities are continually generated and maintained, and where we find subjects – their histories and their interpretations of the world—burdened with agony but productive in hope.

Within such a weighted world, then, "liberating politics" is the dreaming and sentiment, the practice and thinking, which demands and implements, through social movements, egalitarian principles of opportunity *and* liberating empowerment, by and for those who bear imposed social suffering. Such a politics invokes the creativity, resilience and power of those who, as Jacques Rancière writes (1999, 11–12), are "the part that has no part" in social and political systems, those who know an "inclusion" in systems of unequal power, but whose exploitation is also an "exclusion" from truly life-giving empowerment. Such as these deploy art and action to create what social movement activists often term "the people," a coalition of social sufferers whose agency and organizing form blocs of resistance to exploitative systems (Dussel 2008, 71–79). Dussel's carefully theorized notion of "the people" should not be opposed to Hardt and Negri's notion of "the multitude." Both are ways to forge liberating modes of a social and planetary "we."

Liberating Politics Beyond the Good/Evil Binary

A common objection I hear from many US academics is that a liberating politics presumes a simplistic binary of liberation/oppression, and behind it, a grand binary of good and evil. This claim can function as intellectual masking of refusals to acknowledge legitimate demands for liberation. There is, however, a significant concern here: how, to avoid replicating a simplistic binarism, the kind by which US politicos often divide up the world as good and bad, as Cold War voices often have done, foregrounding in imperial rhetoric, for example, "a universal American 'good' and a gendered racial 'Asiatic evil'." (Kim 2010, 38). We might ask, then, what is good and what is evil for a liberating politics, in ways avoiding such binarisms?

Let me here only sketch my approach. Indeed, it is a grander problematic (Taylor 2011, 39–43). Begin with my phrase, "the weight of the world." This weight, recall, is the imposed social suffering from which many seek "the good" of liberation. French philosopher Jean-Luc Nancy writes that the world is always a weighing of bodies—of many types of bodies in relation to one another and in multiple ways. The many practices belonging to human action in the world give structure to this multifarious weighing. Among the multiplicity of interplaying motions, the weighing processes can congeal, and in two major modes. These two are always mutually engaging and shifting in relation to one another, and Nancy terms them "extension" and "concentration" (Nancy 2008, 40–43).

"Extension" is a mode of weighing that preserves a delicately structured, taut relation of the world's bodies to one another. Bodies here weigh such that they balance and orchestrate both intimacy and distance relative to one another. A multiplicity of rhythms is at work in this balance, taking "rhythm" in the broad sense of marking and accenting difference *and* similarity, singularities *and* pluralities. Extension becomes the key ontological trait, indeed a veritable condition for the possibility and realization of, justice, peace, and freedom, for which a liberating politics struggles. Thus, extension is the major way, theoretically, that I would talk about "the good."

What then of "evil"? Extension is always under threat by another dynamic mode in which the world's weighing of bodies congeals. That dynamic is "concentration." It is counterforce to extension and refers to the piling up, cramming, compression of bodies, often as so many cadavers, sometimes as the so-called walking dead in social zones of abandonment. Capital concentrates, says Nancy. Prisons concentrate, as do the global slums. Social hierarchies concentrate, through ranking and constraining.

Such concentration is in contrast to liberating practices of "extension." When facing concentrated powers of antagonism and agony, practices aiming to restore extension offer a kind of "winding cloth" for the mass dead, "to define the spacing of one, and then another" (Nancy 2008, 77). This is no mere marking off of individual from individual, although this *is* crucial: with the winding cloth marking by name, for example, at least some of the increase by hundreds of thousands of Iraqi civilian deaths after the US invasion in 2003 of Iraq. Beyond a distinguishing of individuality, extension as liberating practice also names and foregrounds groups, their lands, and their sites of suffering. They become communities with histories to be named and studied: Guatemala City's ravine barrios, Rio's *favelas,* Gaza's imprisoned Palestinians under lethal and illegal lockdown by Israel, San Francisco's sweatshops of Asian American women workers (Louie 1992). Such sites of suffering are often the fruit of analyzable corporate actors (United Fruit, Jessica McClintock Fashion, Caterpillar, Coca Cola, Bechtel), identifiable protagonists of economic and political displacement. Liberating practice as restoring extension, thus, names corporate powers of concentration, remembers the "souls of the departed," holds them in remembrance, artfully forging rites and social movements for both the living and the dead (Taylor 2011, 199–213).

Distinguishing "concentration" from "extension" becomes for me, then, a way to identify "evil" from "good." Note, however, that this is not another "American binarism." Nor, even in some obverse form, does it embrace a scenario of clearly divided good battling evil forces. Indeed, I do see extension and concentration in opposition, marking what Nancy even terms "brutal collision." But "good" and "evil" are also in tangled relation with one another. Again, differences between "good" and "evil" are matters of the world's congealing, shifts in the modes of bodies' weighing—as extension or concentration. This shifting is comparable, I suggest, to how a single person might "shift" his or her weight from one foot to another, slightly rearranging the body's positions, energies, and parts. Slight as this shift may be, it can determine, somewhat starkly, which of one's two legs or feet bear the most weight. The shifting powers we call good and evil work similarly. Great evils often congeal *in relation to* the mutual intimacy and distancing, the taught balance of bodies and forces of extension, the good. Political theology here will need to be instructed by especially the cultures and religiosities of Asian and Asian American perspectives, as Wonhee Anne Joh does in dialogue with Hae Joon Lee's psychology of Han (Joh 2006, 20–26), for example, wherein good and evil are distinguished but viewed as a complex interplay in ways that the West's more binary viewpoints often find difficult to achieve. Overall, this approach allows us to speak of human being and action as agonistic and antagonistic, always fraught and labile with tension and conflict—here between extension and concentration—while acknowledging also a certain co-belonging of good and evil.

"Transimmanence" in Liberating Politics"

It is amid this agonistic striving between extension and concentration, that transimmanence is important (Nancy 1996, 34–35). It is the key subject-matter of political theology rising from the synergy of arts and social movements. It can reframe the old immanence/transcendence divide that has bedeviled much of Theology. Transimmanence, a dimension of transiting that dwells in human history and practice, especially under conditions of agonistic struggle, is important because the arts can emerge from it with liberating force. Transimmanence is a creative motion found in that deep place of agony in ourselves, personally and collectively, where in relation to social and natural worlds, we know fear, dread, melancholy, and rage. It can take us into despair but just as easily can make us break forth in rebellion and hope. It is prone to a turbulent liminality, a betwixt-and-between milieu of being in which life is always moving, portentously, constituting a spectral haunting, that is, memory bearing threat, demand and promise into the present. It is a place where our affects and practices are suspended between, in struggle amid extension and concentration.

Transimmanence is my rendering of an alternative to transcendence, which yet is no mere anti-transcendence move, being hardly thinkable apart from transcendence (Taylor 2011, 117). Yet, especially when this creative and turbulent force finds expression in the arts, it can be similar to what some seek in discourses of transcendence: a countervailing power against imposed social suffering, but a power that is *within* world and history.

Above, I may have seemed too harsh in judging references to the transcendent as deficient. After all, do not exploited peoples themselves gain leverage for struggle precisely through such reference? I would argue "No, not primarily by pointing to, invoking, 'having' a transcendent, 'God'." The leverage comes in the usage, in its being *artfully made in situations of transimmanence*, with social movements affecting its leverage. Again, it is more the artfulness of the gesture to a transcendent that makes the liberating difference, not the belief or gesture itself. One might turn to notions of "immanent transcendence," which accent the embedded way of the divine in history, in body and in all living. But even here, the primary action and initiative still remain abstracted, attached to something other than those transimmanent places where social movements and arts press for liberating change.

The Liberating Force of Art(s)

It is especially the arts that can highlight the difference between extension and concentration and display the transimmanental way, creating and sustaining the taut, fragile relations of extension that sustain life. In the work of Richard Wright, for example, we find not only a powerful narrative skill, but also a creativity he consciously wields to facilitate this kind of transimmanental motion. As Wright himself wrote, he tried to offer in his art "a scheme of images and symbols whose direction could enlist the sympathies, loyalties and yearning of the millions of Bigger Thomases in every land and race." (Wright 1991, 865). Bigger Thomas, of course, was the main character of Wright's *Native Son,* the racially marked, provoked, at times self-destructive, enlightening figure, caught up in murder and execution. Wright's artful rendering of transimmanental agony is actually hope-making in startling ways, indeed a kind of grotesque but effective "resurrection" amid the primal fear and dread that white supremacism induce (JanMohamed 2005, 288). Theological discourse, especially if it is to be "political theology" as reflection on the arts of liberating struggle, would do well to apprentice itself to the likes of Wright's art and thought.

It is from such spaces of transimmanence, spaces of turbulent liminality bent toward liberating politics, that the arts often break forth and catalyze powerful political movement for change. Moreover, the full liberating effect of art forms depends on social movements, as did the poems from Guantánamo, attaining their public power through efforts of social movements, of their lawyers, publishers, alternative media, and everyday activists (Taylor 2011, 159–187). The synergy between liberating arts and social movements may also center on a song or chant, a dance, or a march.

One can reenvision Christianity's Jesus in terms of art and social movement. A great example would be the reenvisioning of Jesus's "Way of the Cross Procession" in Ana Castillo's *So Far from God*. There, "Loca," a young woman who is the novel's haunting, dying/rising figure, appearing in the final chapter to ride bareback on her horse, Gato Negro, leading a procession like none before. Loca rides as a spiritual guide, accompanied by her mother on foot, with neighbors from women's cooperatives all remembering their losses and hopes. Joined by a "woman singer named Pastora Somebody or Other," the procession winds its way through village and city streets. Jesus, blended artfully with Loca, becomes, in this procession, one whose condemnation to death highlights the dumping of radioactive waste in village sewers, whose cross bearing evokes the suffering of "Native and Hispano families...living below poverty level." Loca, in Castillo's artful telling, conjures new meanings of Jesus and of his procession. Nuclear power plants nail Jesus to the cross. US wars leave Jesus's body limp on the cross, as broken as the story's Latina character lost in Iraq, whose body at novel's end remains unrecovered by the US Army. And—"Ayyy! Jesus died on the cross"—becomes a lament joined to women's crying as "their babies died in their bellies from the poisoning" of pesticides. At end of the procession, Loca departs life to the melancholy tones of a Portuguese *fado* song. As Loca is buried, her mother raises an activist movement, M.O.M.A.S (Mothers of Martyrs and Saints) (Castillo 1993, 238–245).

In previous writing I have followed Nancy in holding these art-forces to have a "prodigious" quality. By "prodigious" I do not mean practices featuring only dramatic, heroic, and iconic action; they are also, just as importantly, "the force" carried in the small everyday activity (*lo cotidiano,* as in Isasi-Díaz 1996, 66–73), the unnoticed, everyday gestures and acts toward justice, an array of artful dealings through many genres (music, novels, sculpture, home décor, tapestry and handcrafts, woodcuts, painting, the novel, the poem). Activism is not just the prerogative of street rally protestors or full-time movement organizers.

Those on the underside of systems of imposed social suffering already display much of this. Note the indigenous peoples in Ecuador organizing their communities against globalization's "free trade" proposals from the United States, and doing so in a form of Pentecostal Christian practice taken to the streets in artful marching and creative presentation. That mix of community organizing and Pentecostal spirit for radical political effect surprises people who define groups only by theological beliefs' "liberal" or "conservative" traits. Or, consider feminist activists of many backgrounds who continue to work in communities with patriarchal ways, but do so by artfully turning practices in ways that subvert patriarchs' power in those communities.

Nancy has a great line I offer here, summarizing the role of the artful image in transimmanental movements such as these: "The image," he writes, "is the prodigious force-sign of an improbable presence irrupting from the heart of a restlessness on which nothing can be built." In short, concentration may "weigh down" the world with structures that cram, pile, amass bodies, but ultimately nothing can hold back the deep restlessness that creates something new, an "improbable presence" carried by forces of popular art and social movement.

Conclusion: Theological Discourse Beyond the Guild

In conclusion I respond to what surely some in Christian guild Theology may ask: what about the particular doctrinal notions of "God," "Jesus," the notions of "Church," "Spirit," and so on. Such notions I would not simply jettison, as indicated by my example of Jesus in Castillo's novel. I am suggesting, however, especially if we are asking about the publicness of theological discourse, that the traditional symbols be reimagined in a different paradigm. They are best reinterpreted not through the paradigm of doctrinal language referencing a transcendent, but through one that analyses the transimmanental art-force of liberating politics in social movements. Indeed, I suggest that theological discourses have already migrated, as it were, well beyond the guilds of "Theology," though working in the margins of university divinity schools and religion departments, giving rise to public and political theology at work in transdisciplinary academies and public institutions. Usually these sites attend to the agonistic processes of struggle around notions of race, gender, sexuality, and class—*especially analyzed* from intercultural and counter-colonial perspectives. Poets, artists, and activists figure as special beacons for theory and theology. Amid agony and hope, they signal the dimensions into which political theologians, reflecting on arts of liberating politics, best enter. Richard Wright and Ana Castillo, cited in this essay, are but two exemplars. So also is Eddy Zheng of this chapter's epigraph. There are of course a myriad of others: novelists Leslie Marmon Silko (*Almanac of the Dead*), or Ha Jin (*War Trash*), or poets Suji Kwock Kim (*Notes from a Divided Country*), Martín Espada (*Poetry like Bread*), Janice Mirikitani (*Shedding Silence*), and June Jordan (*Kissing God Good-bye*). And these are just the novelists and the poets; a wide range of other art forms can be vibrant with the art-force of liberation. From the likes of these and more, theology itself, and again not just political theology, finds public voice—beyond the guild.

Notes

1. On Zheng and his activism, see http://eddyzhengstory.com/.
2. For a splendid collection on race in political theology, see Lloyd 2012.
3. US attacks on Iran's facilities have already occurred (Sanger 2012).
4. Not cited in Taylor: Mignolo 2011, 62–65.

References

Alexander, Michelle. 2010. *The New Jim Crow: Mass Incarceration in the Age of Colorblindness*. New York: The New Press.

Benítez-Rojo, Antonio. 1996. *The Repeating Island: The Caribbean and the Postmodern Perspective*. 2nd edition. Durham and London: Duke University Press.

Castillo, Ana. 1993. *So Far from God*. New York: W. W. Norton.

Crockett, Clayton and Jeffrey W. Robbins. 2012. *Religion, Politics and the Earth: The New Materialism*. New York: Palgrave Macmillan.

De Vries, Hent and Lawrence Sullivan. 2006. *Political Theologies: Public Religions in a Post-Secular World*. New York: Fordham University Press.

Dussel, Enrique. 2008. *Twenty Theses on Politics*. Durham and London: Duke University Press.

Ellacuría, Ignacio. 1973. *Teología política*. San Salvador: Ediciones del Secretariado Social Interdiocesano.

Farmer, Paul. 2003. *Pathologies of Power: Health, Human Rights and the New War on the Poor*. Berkeley: University of California Press.

Hardt, Michal and Antonio Negri. 2009. *Commonwealth*. Cambridge, MA: Harvard University Press.

Isasi-Díaz, Ada María. 1996. *Mujerista Theology: A Theology for the Twenty-First Century*. Maryknoll, NY: Orbis Books.

JanMohamed, Abdul R. 2005. *The Death-Bound Subject: Richard Wright's Archaeology of Death*. Durham and London: Duke University Press.

Joh, Wonhee Anne. 2006. *Heart of the Cross: A Postcolonial Christology*. Nashville, TN: Westminster John Knox Press.

Kahn, Paul W. 2011. *Political Theology: Four New Chapters on the Concept of Sovereignty*. New York: Columbia University Press.

Kim, Jodi. 2010. *Ends of Empire: Asian American Critique and the Cold War*. Minneapolis: University of Minnesota Press.

Kwok, Pui-lan and Jeorg Rieger. 2012. *Occupy Religion: Theology of the Multitude*. Lanham, MD: Rowman and Littlefield.

Lloyd, Vincent W. 2012, ed. *Race and Political Theology*. Stanford, CA: Stanford University Press.

Louie, Miriam Ching. 1992. "Immigrant Asian Women in Bay Area Garment Sweat Shops." *AmerAsia Journal* 18.1: 1–26.

Mignolo, Walter D. 2011. *The Darker Side of Modernity*. Durham and London: Duke University Press.

Nancy, Jean-Luc. 1996, 1994. *The Muses*. Translated by Peggy Kamuf. Stanford, CA: Stanford University Press.

———. 2007. *The Creation of the World, Or Globalization*. Albany: SUNY Press.

———. 2008. *Corpus*. Translated by Richard A. Rand. New York: Fordham University Press.

Nguyen, Tram. 2005. *We Are All Suspects Now: Untold Stories from Immigrant Communities after 9/11*. Boston: Beacon Press.

Quijano, Aníbal. 2000. "Coloniality of Power, Ethnocentrism and Latin America." *Nepantla* 1.3: 533–80.

Rancière, Jacques. 1999. *Disagreement: Politics and Philosophy*. Translated by Julie Rose. Minneapolis: University of Minnesota Press.

Sanger, David. 2012. *Confront and Conceal: Obama's Secret War and Surprising Use of American Power*. New York: Crown Publishers.

Sharma, Nitasha Tamar. 2010. *Hip Hop Desis: South Asian American, Blackness and Global Race Consciousness*. Durham, NC: Duke University Press.

Sung, Jung Mo. 2011. *The Subject, Capitalism and Religion: Horizons of Hope in Complex Societies*. New York: Palgrave Macmillan.

Taylor, Mark Lewis. 2005. *Religion, Politics and the Christian Right: Post-9/11 Powers and American Empire*. Minneapolis, MN: Fortress Press.

———. 2011. *The Theological and the Political: On the Weight of the World*. Minneapolis, MN: Fortress Press.

———. 2008. "Empire and Transcendence: Hardt and Negri's Challenge to Theology and Ethics." In *Evangelicals and Empire: Christian Alternatives to the*

Political Status Quo, edited by Bruce Ellis Benson and Peter Goodwin Heltzel. Grand Rapids, MI: Brazos Press.

Wright, Richard. 1991. *Richard Wright: Early Works*. Washington, DC: Library of America.

Zheng, Eddy. 2007. "Autobiography@33." In *Other: An Asian & Pacific Islander Prisoners' Anthology*, edited by Eddy Zheng. The Asian Prisoner Support Committee. San Leandro, CA: Dakota Press.

PART III

The Significance of
Fuerzas Para La Lucha
(God-Given Strength for the Struggle)

CHAPTER 9

Naming What We Want: Thoughts on Religious Vocabulary and the Desire for Quality of Life

Anthony B. Pinn

President Obama's inauguration address briefly mapped out a geography of belonging that included a fuller range of religious and philosophical perspectives running from nontheists to theists. To the extent that it forced a momentary reckoning with the competing life orientation claims lodged in the United States, this "opening up" has been of some value. Yet, it did little to address the vocabulary and grammar used to shape and present the sense of "life, liberty, and happiness" operative in so many quarters. How does one present "life, liberty, and happiness" within the context of competing faith claims with differing perspectives on, for example, the nature of the humans who are undertaking such pursuits and claiming these rights? For instance, much of the undergirding thought for these pursuits and claims rest on a soft theism; yet, what is the "look" of this pursuit (and the nature of happiness) when not buttressed by theism but instead by the "non-belief," as President Obama put it, of some citizens?

In this essay, I make an effort to address such questions through a centering of embodied life, the meaning of our occupation of time and space, as the framework of discussions concerning the nature of existence defined by "life, liberty, and the pursuit of happiness." As a nation, we have mapped out the geography for and content of life with respect to the activities and conversations that promote pleasure; and we have made this configuration a basic right associated with citizenship. What remains a persistent issue is public discussion concerning the markers of the pleasurable: what is the proper language for describing it?

Developments in the public, political debate in the United States over the past several years point not only to the continuing dilemma of race (and class) in this country, but also suggest the inadequate connection between the traditional grammar of political obligation and opportunity, and the "look" of our political wants and needs. That is to say, for instance, the Tea Party and other modalities of political and "moral" recalibration seek to use a strict and restricting grammar of Christian obligation as a way of framing the content and intent of, say, the US Constitution. Claiming to represent the spirit and purpose of liberty and freedom that have defined this country and were symbolized by the Boston Tea Party, contemporary "tea partiers" promote a conservative view of US internal and external dealings. While maintaining the pretense of openness to all committed to the welfare of this nation, regardless of race, religion, and so on, their framing of the Tea Party's meaning and work, and their framing of the United States as a nation is premised on a language and grammar that uses the Christian faith as the basic conceptual paradigm. This is their language, their grammar, because they assert that we *are* a Christian nation.

Although gaining some attention within political circles, the Tea Party Movement does not capture the full imagination of US citizens; yet, the appeal to Christian vocabulary and grammar as a way to articulate and translate basic principles of the US self-understanding pushes beyond this movement and is much older than it. Assuming this language of the Christian faith should, and has always, marked the intent and self-understanding of this nation, politicians and citizens from various political camps agree at least in soft (self-serving) ways that it should persist. Yet, it hasn't worked well; it has never worked well in that this language—the vision of collective life supported by this language—has not safeguarded the welfare of the collective community in all its diversity.

The Christian language is too narrow, too "cosmic" and not grounded enough to serve as a way to organize the energy and needs of the United States, too narrow to give full and earthy meaning to "life, liberty, and the pursuit of happiness" that defines so much of our self-understanding in this nation. The Christian faith, and its language by extension, is too grounded in a glance beyond this world; it seeks its meaning and approval beyond the confines of human history. In short, at its core, it is "other-worldly," and how can that type of language give full meaning to rather worldly—property inspired—concerns? We stand in need of a different way of speaking about the deepest desires of this nation, because those desires and wants are ultimately tied to physicality, to the material nature of our selves, as opposed to being responsive to any type of spiritual or transcendent qualities.

Here's the problem: appeal to Christian language tends to assume our basic desires as individuals within the context of a national community drawn from a relationship to transcendent concerns and meanings. However, the meaning of life, liberty, and happiness are actually biological, neurological—neurobiological—and not easily captured through traditional theological assumptions. Traditional Christian theology—think what one hears in most churches—points in the wrong direction in that it takes focus off humans as simply biological creatures and seeks to frame them as something more significant, creators with a divine spark and purpose.

Even more worldly forms of theological thinking that begin to emerge during the late nineteenth and twentieth century with figures such as Rev. Walter Rauschenbusch and later Dr. Martin L. King Jr., are concerned with the world, but still view it as a somewhat imperfect resemblance to a more perfect cosmic reality that we must seek to secure. Their liberal theology—or social gospel—sought to model human interactions on the model of Jesus Christ, thereby giving Christians a way of addressing pressing issues of modern life by following the principles of Jesus's ministry. But even this points backwards and understands the best of human want and human capacity as tied to a cosmic relationship. It fails to recognize the limited and deeply earthbound nature of human want, desires, and pursuits. There is still in place the assumption that earthly activities are connected to unseen dramas and struggles—"powers and principalities"—impacting human life. This is not to say that figures such as King didn't appreciate human ethics and social structures; rather it is to say that he still understood these things to be tied to transhistorical concerns and possibilities. It is premised on the assumption that there is something out there, something that is concerned with us and in relationship to whom we have described and arranged the workings and rules of our national life.

This way of thinking about our basic aims as citizens of the United States has not served us well. It has ignored the real source of these desires for life, liberty, and happiness because it cast them as having some type of cosmic origin and function when, actually, they are merely the result of our biology. We won't develop a useful and productive way of discussing the nature and function of these three desires if we don't first gain clarity concerning their relationship to who (or what) we are as biologically motivated creatures. Such a turn might give us a better way of understanding the motivations for the central importance of and meaning behind our guiding principles and ethics. And in better understanding them, we might be better equipped to safeguard their importance and opportunities to secure them.

Recent studies that take complex neuroscience findings and make them available to a general public point out the complexities of our brain—the manner in which it actually holds within its mysteries the source of so much we once associated with spiritual essence and the like. This is to suggest, as *The Believing Brain* (Shermer 2011) makes clear, these things are all a matter of belief; yet, these beliefs have no substantive metaphysical basis. They are still a part of our biology and should be addressed as such. The real basis for our commonality, for our shared commitments, is not religiously grounded in any traditional sense—too many religious orientations in the United States for that—but instead is the result of shared biology: the brain shapes and monitors these desires and pursuits and it is this biological relatedness that ties all humans together. The working of the brain as geography for this structuring of the meaningful life is the shared basis for our guiding principles and their hold on us. Hence, the language we use to describe and explain these principles should be tied not to a particular religion but to the workings of our shared humanity.

Theology traditionally understood and arranged as a language for particular religious orientations is too limited and limiting for a proper sense of our fundamental pursuits that ground the quality of life. While transcendent forces might offer a convenient way of solidifying the authority of particular ideas, notions of God(s) do not adequately represent the shared "stuff" of human motivation for the safeguarding of the three principles noted so many times already in this brief piece. The cosmic script offered through God(s) seldom changes in substantial ways, although human need and self-understanding do change. And while there may be something genetic about our religiosity as many philosophers and scientists now note, this does not mean that a particular arrangement of this inclination beyond a general quest for profound life meaning should rule the day.

Our life framing principles are about meaning—the fostering of meaning through the framing of what most matters—but we should not attempt to describe or understand this in ways that downplay our biology. Our neurobiology, the fleshy nature of our humanity, is the source of our inclinations whether they are political, cultural, social, spiritual, and so on. We should be mindful of this when we think about and seek to formulate the mechanisms for accessing and securing the "stuff" of our individual existence as the substance of our rights as citizens. To say that these things are God-given is not to point to something beyond ourselves, but to simply suggest that they are an outgrowth of our very biology—a dimension of our fundamental structure, and this is what makes them compelling and long lasting on the group level.

Turning again to *The Believing Brain* (Shermer 2011), there is reason to believe that the brain—or in general the physical workings of the human—is responsible for our political inclinations and all their trappings, including the guiding politico-social arrangements of life such as the principles of life, liberty, and the pursuit of happiness. This being the case, no one religious grammar garnered from one of the dominant religious communions in the United States is adequate for speaking to or for the struggle regarding our deep yearning for these principles active within the context of both our individual lives and our communal existence. Hence, while religious orientation and belief structures may prove useful for the individual and the like-minded, they do not provide a language adequate as the mode of exchange within the public arena.

Our challenge is to actually develop such a language, to gather such a grammar and vocabulary. It requires at the very least tolerance, imagination, and a different perspective on difference. This is not to say that religious commitment and theological vocabulary serve no purpose. They do, within certain confined dimensions of private (and communal) life. However, they are not expansive enough, do not capture enough of the landscape of life in the United States, to constitute the most viable way of naming and speaking about the goals of civic existence marked out within the context of an expansive national community. Such is the case because, as Benedict Anderson rightly notes, this national community is not based on direct contact but rather on imagined connections, and these imagined connections cannot be defined by the workings of one particular theistic faith stance (Anderson 1983). In fact, our understanding of shared human need and desire isn't solved through understanding the workings of religion, but rather through a more profound understanding of how the brain works. This is because religion is just one product of the brain at work. And, it isn't necessarily the most significant product because it demonizes our biological selves.

Instead, a more humanistic approach to what is meant by life, liberty, and the pursuit of happiness is helpful in that it centers the human—as material and cultural reality. These three, in a general sense, have something to do with pleasure—how it is understood, shaped, and captured. And while various religious traditions might have a troubled relationship with pleasure, particularly the way in which it is dependent on the body that some traditions hold suspect as the site of all our troubles, pleasure and the desire for it are deeply human and components of individual and collective notions of fulfillment. Navigation of the pathways of pleasure—the structuring and safeguarding of pleasure—is part of our wiring. It is fundamentally human, and is more basic than the teachings or language of any particular religious language or tradition. These principles or "unalienable rights" are promoted in the Declaration of Independence as cornerstones of the pleasure of freedom. They belong to each person across an expansive geography of communities. How, then, can such far-reaching and fundamental rights be adequately defined and captured? Do they not require the conversation and exchange made possible by a more fundamental, a more humanistic, grammar—one that centers on the commonalities of our basic shared biology over against the irresolvable differences of theistic belief?

What I propose involves a clear dilemma—a need to recognize the possibility of tension between theistic readings of these three desires and nontheistic perceptions of the same. After all, both positions involve belief. Yet, I make a pitch for the nontheistic variety of belief in that theisms tend not to be institutionally and theologically flexible enough to shift quickly (or in real time) with expansion in knowledge. They are too rigid, not plastic enough. The response of so many religious communities to the demands for gay rights and productions under the law serves as just one example of what I mean. Pleasure, as *The Compass of Pleasure* makes clear, is tied to our brain chemistry and part of our neurophysiology (Linden 2011). Theism speaks to and about pleasure and makes an effort to forge a language for understanding and controlling it, but in rather truncated ways—ways that do not fully appreciate just how "earthbound" are both religion and pleasure. To have public discussions concerning pleasure outlined by "life, liberty, and the pursuit of happiness" requires a more expansive set of tools than those offered by Christianity or any other theistic tradition. Needed are mechanisms of exchange more consciously stemming from an understanding of humanity as central and with less appeal to transcendence.

And here I repeat much of what I said in two *Religion Dispatches* articles from October 27, 2009 and February 13, 2009. To the extent that it is possible (and many atheists will reject this suggestion), attention should be given to a search for common ethical ground that brackets the harsher presentations of both theistic and atheistic views. I am not asking for a "can't we all get along" rejection of debate and a suspension of aggressive wrestling over ideas. It is important to challenge beliefs as a way of safeguarding human accountability and integrity; but there must also be a push for more than destruction of all markers of religious commitment. Atheists should continue to interrogate and critique theistic orientations, and adherents of theistic positions should continue to challenge atheists. If not, careful and self-critical attention paid to science by some atheists, for instance, could easily become scientism—a faith of its own, with figures such as Richard Dawkins serving as its prophets.

History shows that reason may alter the posture of faith-based communities, may force them to shift their language and limit their size and their sociopolitical reach, but it will not destroy faith. The very definition of faith should make this apparent. Atheists miscalculate the core significance of theism if they assume it is about doctrine and creeds, ritual forms and physical structures; things most often attacked. Theism, at its core, is about the making of meaning and the establishment of stories and practices related to how and why we occupy time and space; ritual, doctrines, sacred texts and so on are only cultural manifestations of this deeper meaning. These rituals and doctrines are secondary, not primary: they are modified; they shift; they change to fit the historical-cultural context. Attacks on theism's theological or ritual shortcomings, while correct in some regards, will not end theism.

Theism and atheism/humanism will persist, and any real gain we make toward healthy existence for our world must involve collaboration (not assimilation) and partnerships between moderates within both groups. This is not denial of difference and doesn't require rejection of one's chosen orientation. Rather, it involves recognition that a mature approach to life rejects fundamentalism of any kind, and demands complex relationships of shared ethical commitment even when those relationships are burdened with tension. But the more difficult task involves development of the national posture necessary for achieving this vision. The problem is obvious; religious traditions involve competing faith claims, conflicting postures toward the practice of faith, and shifting assumptions concerning the public nature of religious commitment. Rich, "thick," and complex discourse requires new structures, new rules of engagement—a push beyond what marks the current and public framing of religious concerns and practices. Great care must be exercised, or what we will get is superficial "tolerance" of religious humanists and secularists, a sense of what it means to be religious in the United States that barely hides an assumed theistic, if not Christian, backstory.

President Obama's call for recognition of religious diversity falls short, in that little thus far suggests a rethinking of how we in the United States define, arrange, and shape our fundamental concerns. There will be no questioning of our general assumptions concerning what is meant when the United States is referred to as a religious nation. There is an opportunity here that should not be missed. Rather than simply assuming a clear understanding of what it means to be "American" and "religious," here is a chance to interrogate the wide range of possibilities. This involves sustained examination of what it means (and what must be surrendered) to embrace all modalities of religion within the context of this democracy. The signs of a morally and ethically centered and successful nation might need some rethinking in light of the various (and at times competing) norms held dear and celebrated within the context of our religious diversity. For the type of growth I suggest here, the nation will need a task force charged with helping politicians and civic leaders to think about the nature and meaning of our nation's religious diversity. This group of scholars and leaders (both theistic and nontheistic) would be charged with developing a framework for addressing the intersections of public life by helping foster a language and posture for engagement in public conversation concerning the pleasures that matter to us most.

References

Anderson, Benedict. 1983. *Imagined Communities: Reflections on the Origin and Spread of Nationalism*. London and New York: Verso Books.

Linden, David J. 2011. *The Compass of Pleasure: How Our Brains Make Fatty Foods, Orgasm, Exercise, Marijuana, Generosity, Vodka, Learning, and Gambling Feel So Good*. New York: Viking.

Pinn, Anthony. 2009. "Atheists Gather in Burbank: A Humanist's Response." *Religion Dispatches*, October 27.

Pinn, Anthony. 2009. "O(Pinn)ion: Reevaluating a Faith-Based Nation." *Religion Dispatches*, February 13.

Shermer, Michael. 2011. *The Believing Brain: From Ghosts and Gods to Politics and Conspiracies—How We Construct Beliefs and Reinforce Them as Truths*. New York: Henry Holt.

CHAPTER 10

Redeeming Equality: Life, Liberty, and Alternatives to Obliviousness

Mary McClintock Fulkerson

Some of our favorite values as Americans come from one of our most inspirational founding documents, *The Declaration of Independence.* Who would not wish to be "independent" from dominating sovereign powers? And who would not treasure such values as "equality" and "inalienable rights"—especially the rights of "life, liberty," and the freedom to pursue "happiness"? Since early on, when the process of forging a new nation highlighted contrasts with the monarchical hierarchies of the rest of the world, the claim that we are all "equal" has long been a source of pride for the United States. More recently, we celebrate this value as we compare ourselves to contemporary authoritarian regimes such as Libya, North Korea, and Syria, or to what we take to be the outrageous patriarchies in some Muslim countries. In the United States, by contrast, we *are all equal*—of the same status—or so say our official documents.

Of course history does not completely support our zealous pride with regard to these claims. Multiple residents on American soil have had problems gaining equality. The legal refusal to recognize Africans brought here through the transatlantic slave market as anything but property is an obvious and embarrassing contradiction of our boasts. So are the ongoing terrible treatment of Latina/o "immigrants" and the way as a nation we dealt and continue to deal with Native Americans—as if

Euro-Americans were not immigrants. The very authors of our inspirational founding documents and a number of the "Founding Fathers" themselves lived this contradiction. Thomas Jefferson owned slaves, as did George Washington, James Madison, John Hancock, and Patrick Henry, among others. The problem is still broader. For example women, regardless of race, were long denied official full citizenship.

The deeper challenge, however, is not simply the fact that the "we" envisioned as a nation "under God" did not include everyone. I will return to what it might mean to be "under God," something that gets overlooked in typical assessments of our self-image is the complex *dynamics* of exclusion and what that suggests about the roots of exclusion. One common explanation of these contradictions between asserted values and actual practices is the idea of inevitable progress. In short, the argument goes, the fathers had a vision; and even if they did not live it out with complete consistency in the beginning, that vision would inevitably come to pass. Each generation, you might say, has a clearer moral vision than the preceding one. Thus, along with "life, liberty, and the pursuit of happiness," *inevitable progress* is part of the American story.

An example contradicting this explanatory theme in our national narrative, however, would be the Supreme Court's stunning retreat from what appeared to be clear and logical progress made when the post–Civil War society recognized this wrongly excluded population. The faithful development of the American Dream—"American values"—*seemed* to win the day with the post–Civil War Reconstruction Era. In 1868, the Fourteenth Amendment granted citizenship and equal protection to *all persons born or naturalized in the United States, thereby including* African Americans. In 1870, the Fifteenth Amendment granted Black men the right to vote. Soon after 1875, a Civil Rights Act granted equal accommodation to all in "inns, public conveyances . . . and other places of public amusement." In just a few years, however, these crucial next steps in the logical expansion of "life, liberty and the pursuit of happiness" were radically undermined. Civil Rights Cases in 1883 overturned this democratic access to public places (Civil Rights Act of 1875), and soon after that the court hierarchalized "equality" with what we now call the "separate but equal" of *Plessey v. Ferguson* (1896). While "separate but equal" referred specifically to railroad accommodations, it quickly spread. Progress requiring the logical expansion of liberty for all not only did not happen, things actually went backward.

When given another look, a second narration of our mistakes suggests that something even deeper than slacking off is behind the sometimes bumpy road toward delivery of our values for all. "Separate but equal," "Jim Crow," and segregation of every sort have long been over, or so goes this argument. Viewing Blacks as less than human, refusing them the right to own property or vote, not allowing persons gendered "female" to vote or own property—these are egregious traditions and are now viewed as unjust by the majority of Americans. Most of us think of them as sins of the *past*, long gone and adequately addressed by legislation. Discrimination, so goes this narrative, is no longer real, precisely because the desegregation and antidiscrimination laws that prohibit unfair treatment of persons on account of race or gender are finally in place. In short, legal changes have fixed these problems, and, with regard to what appears to be the most egregious displays of exclusion, except for crazies like the Ku Klux Klan, the majority of Americans are simply not "racist" anymore. (Another conversation, of course, is awareness of our "sexist" and "heterosexist" cultures.) So widespread is this view that our contemporary situation is typically narrated as the age of "colorblindness." Numerous Americans—mostly white—proudly say something like, "I don't see color, just people." While this narration is often focused on the "Black-white" binary of marginalization, folks typically assume colorblindness denies a real spectrum of ethnic othering.

Exclusion and Obliviousness

According to these two common accounts, exclusions are a form of old-fashioned ignorance that our more enlightened generations inevitably outgrow, or exclusions are a form of old-fashioned explicit and horrific bigotry that has been solved by legislation—a set of wrongs that our "colorblind" nation has clearly moved beyond. Both narratives ignore the deep complexity of exclusion. Both seem to assume that exclusion is about mistaken ideas and ignorance, or a long-outdated display of malicious prejudice. In fact, however, I would argue that deeply embedded postures such as racism, sexism, and other "isms" are not resolved by progressive rationality, the emergence of basically "good" people; nor are they fixed with antidiscrimination laws alone. For example, the contemporary mantra of "colorblindness" does not indicate that the deeply embedded residuals of racism and ethnoracism (Alcoff 2011) have not been adequately addressed, either in their legal or their post-segregation forms. Neighborhoods and religious communities remain largely racially segregated (Edwards 2008); significant gaps in income, education and such between whites and so-called racial groups continue—and groups besides African Americans are at risk. Many scholars have analyzed colorblindness as a form of avoidance, indeed, they call it the new form of "racism" (Bonilla-Silva 2010; Emerson and Yancey 2011).

What complicates exclusion has to do with a kind of obliviousness. Obliviousness is not a literal blindness defined as the failure to see something or someone. Rather, it is typically connected to deeply internalized, pre-reflective habits and images that characterize "others," typically those who are "different" from us (whoever "we" are). Those habits have to do with affective and preconscious, rather than "rational" reactions—often from fear of difference. Reactions are multiple; the other can be perceived as simply odd, as insignificant, or as threatening, resulting in shared images that "typify" the other. Most importantly, these images have to do with what kind of bodies appear "normal" to one's group, including which bodies are perceived as authorized, legitimate wielders of power. Since fear of the "other"—those not like "us"—is a human reaction, not simply the stereotyping done by one group, what really matters is a group's social power to enforce its images of the other in the wider society. A less powerful group is thus not innocent of such othering (even with added justification), it simply has less ability to enact it.

While theories of the role of power and interest in shaping our worldviews and attendant blindnesses are multiple, then, at the very least, we can say that exclusions are rooted in an obliviousness that entails deeply habituated *aversiveness* to the so-called other. Such aversiveness and accompanying stereotyping images can render the other as less than fully human, such as the Euro-centric colonialists' view of the African American as property. Aversiveness and the negative images produced can also be internalized by marginalized groups in the form of self-hatred, as evidenced by the valorizing of "whiteness" in Latino/a as well as African American communities (Padilla 2001). With the intersections of marginalizing and *privileging* markers come complicated versions of perceiving the other as a subordinate version of the properly human, such as patriarchal views of women. In certain periods the "domestic" for white women was symbolized as a kind of "pedestal." This granted white women a certain kind of "status"—especially compared to women designated as having "race" or lower class—even as being on a pedestal prohibited their access to public agency and power.

Obliviousness, then, is not simply an accidental overlooking of those characterized as "other," a literal blindness of sorts. Nor is it always a conscious dislike of the other. Obliviousness entails a kind of aversion that typically comes to consciousness when the other is experienced as being "out of place," or having stepped "over the line." The white master did not necessarily even notice the slave unless he/she transgressed the expected submissive posture, and the old mantra "don't look a white man in the eye" has held sway long after slavery. Even now there are folks who honor women, *unless* those female bodies transgress their proper place by, say, stepping into a pulpit to preach. A typically pre-reflective affective attitude, the sensibility of aversiveness may not be explicitly hateful, but it still dehumanizes or constricts the other.

Our history of exclusions offers illustrations of the way such obliviousness is displayed in myths that help to "naturalize" the views of those in power. The centuries-old triumphalistic mantra that Christopher Columbus "discovered" American in 1492, is not just an intellectual error or a visual mistake. It was and is a colonialist *myth*—exposed as such when we recognize that this so-called discovered land was inhabited for centuries by various tribes we now call Native Americans. More accurately, Columbus and the subsequent onrush of European travelers *invaded* a geographical territory already honored and sustained by inhabitants. The way we have interpreted what Columbus did has validated the enduring colonialist posture toward Native peoples and obviously rings hollow with the equality of all because these human beings and their rich cultures were not recognized as such. The continuing appeal by conservatives to the "traditional" or "biblical family" to prevent legalization of same-sex marriage is a more contemporary narrative that falsifies history. For many many years, marriage was available only for whites, women (regardless of "race") were conceived as property, many lower-class women and children of all races were factory workers rather than happy residents in nuclear "domestic" families. The last place the so-called traditional nuclear family appears is in the Bible, where model men of faith were polygamous, often had concubines, and the savior was a single guy who never settled down. These examples remind us that the very concept of "all men" in "all men are created equal" is a false universal that covers up aversiveness toward certain kinds of bodies, construing them as less than fully human.

Of course, there is also an ironic honesty in the early use of "all men are created equal" that illustrates assumptions underlying what counted as "normal." As noted, women, regardless of "race," literally did not qualify for two centuries of that phrase's use, that is, they were not considered equal. It was not until 1920 that women were granted the vote. And while racially there were vast differences between the access to "rights," sources of protection and well-being for women designated "white" and for those viewed as "Black" or "Negro," from the beginning the marker "woman" was disabling for all, though not in the same manner. Ironically, the phrase "all men" continues to be used, with regard to rights and equality, ignoring that it is a false universal. A practice allowing one group—whites, and mostly white men—to function as "the normative human" is a practice based upon dominance by that group and discomfort, fear, or aversiveness for the image of the other kind of body as voter, or leader, or authoritative figure. This practice signals an aversiveness that is not completely cured, but simply less public today. Indeed, potential candidates for the Republican Party's presidential nomination in 2012 have included women. But such aversiveness still exists, even in complicated forms, as illustrated by candidate Michelle Bachmann's celebration of her submissiveness to her husband.

What will "redeem" the realities of exclusion, especially if I am right that the latter entail deeply internalized marginalizing stereotypes that contribute to aversiveness? If the inevitability of "progress" or increased rationality does not "fix" such aversiveness, what revitalization of American values might help? As a theologian, my interest is in the potential of religious themes for addressing these harms. While the last thing we need is a move toward Christianizing the nation, there are other ways to recognize the public value of religious faiths and traditions than reproducing religion, ways that can resonate deeply with the theme of justice for all. I now turn to a potential twist in our God-centered rhetoric that might just resonate, namely, the value of *iconoclasm*.

One Nation Under God: Invitation to Self-Criticism

The US theme of "One nation under God" uses explicitly religious language, but does *not* need to be heard as a requirement to belong to a specific religion or to any religion at all. While, admittedly, that will likely be a hard sell, I propose that such discourse can invite those of us who are religious to link our commitment to justice and equality for all to *iconoclasm*, defined as the refusal to absolutize—to make an "idol" of—any human identity or social arrangement. Some would argue that belief in God directs our attention away from the world and undermines radical care for material reality. This is a legitimate criticism. However, this other "condition" of the God-relation—iconoclasm—has the potential to do something very different, even to aid and enhance radical care for the world in a particular way.

At its best, worshipping God entails the refusal to grant any worldly thing—a tradition, a social identity, even a religion—a permanent, unquestionable status, especially insofar as such "idolatries" inevitably engender harm toward the "outsider," who can be perceived as a potential threat to your false security. Refusal to absolutize worldly entities is *not* identical with escape from the finitely good creation; it is about a self-critical way to honor and engage it, that is, *self-criticism in the name of justice*. The iconoclasm inherent in "One nation under God" could thus be read as recognition of the necessity for ongoing self-criticism as key to a national identity, an identity crucially defined around liberty for *all*. So linked the insistence on "for all" in our founding documents can become a crucial reminder not only of the inevitability of prejudice, that is, that fallibility and blindness are inevitable features of humanity regardless of one's status, but also that those with power are able to enact their prejudice in more harmful ways. Consequently, iconoclasm should hold us regularly accountable, especially those of us who are religious, when we appeal to our visionary values, requiring that we ask how our interests and values may be excluding and harming other groups.

Taking iconoclasm or "self-criticism in the name of justice" as fundamental to our national identity provides a rich way to *reread* our historical narratives, at least for those who are religious. It requires a corrective to the false valorizations of who counted—or counts—as "us." The earlier cited examples of exclusiveness referred to official discourse and myths/narratives of the nation, and not to fixed accounts of "what really happened." Whether documented or not, indigenous peoples have always had agency and history, as have other ignored or marginalized groups. There have always been activists from both marginalized and dominant populations who have stood up for excluded/oppressed groups. For example, predominantly white Quakers created the first document protesting slavery in 1688; white Americans created an abolition movement that eventually helped bring slavery down. Women of all races have always "acted up," and we might more accurately say that the first feminists were indigenous women. "Self-criticism in the name of justice," then requires that "official" history be rewritten precisely to display the "equality"—the full value—of all.

The sometimes productive function of religious traditions as they intersect with such values as life, liberty, and equality can thus be recognized in a rewritten American history around the agency of ignored populations. While iconoclasm may not have been explicitly invoked for this rewriting, it can serve to label exclusively male white history as idolatrous. "Redemption" of history includes such figures as the Grimke sisters, Sojourner Truth, Maria Steward, Jarena Lee (b. 1783), Elizabeth Cady Stanton, Lucy Stone, Susan B. Anthony, Anna Julia Cooper (1858–1964), and Ella Baker (1906–1986), who creatively used these intersections of religion with national values to broaden women's access to the public sphere. Believing that Christianity was in essence a religion that values all individuals, in a country founded on such principles as "no government, no taxation, without representation," these women found the status quo of the nineteenth century (where women could not vote, or be educated, or own property if married, and *were* property if African American) intolerable. The history of Black America is now being rewritten to take seriously African American women activists, who, although not typically named, were crucial to the racial justice revolutions in this country. A civil rights activist, lawyer, and later the first African American woman Episcopal priest, Pauli Murray, for example, not only saw real connections between Christian symbols and expansion of American justice for African Americans, she coined the phrase "Jane Crow" to indicate that antiracism movements need to address sexism as well, which for Murray included heterosexism (Azaransky 2011).

In short, a primary American value that can potentially contribute to correcting historic exclusions is iconoclasm, a form of self-critique. Admittedly, this will be seen as a disruptive read of one nation "under God," for historically "One nation under God" has legitimized tyranny, not required ongoing self-criticism. "Under God" can and has been interpreted as divine *authorization* of whatever those in power want to do. However, such views qualify as idolatry—false worship. A *self-critical* national vision valorizing inalienable rights for all might help address the problem of exclusion because iconoclasm-wedded-to-justice recognizes that achievement of perfection, of an identity that is free of all fear and attendant blindness/aversion, is simply not a human possibility. Such fear is the underside of hubris, and willingness to self-inspect and "confess" our inevitable unjust practices is the only way, at least for religious communities, to begin to address our fallibility and the blindnesses that accompany it. And this self-criticism supports a rich and vibrant ongoing revision of our history, a rewriting that should never come to an end.

Justice for All: The Public Good

A second relevant American value, invoked in "justice for all" would enhance what is implicit in the value of rewriting our history based upon *iconoclasm in the interest of justice.* Expanding our history only happens if we *care* about previously unrecognized others, especially the "we" who are most privileged; it is about broadening our sense of the public good, which entails a communal "we." (Remember *e pluribus unum*—"out of many one.") This value is only "implicit" in the concern to revise history because the value of the public good, invoked in our mantra "justice for all," as a sense of who we are as we the people and accountability, is often undermined by an obsessive focus on individualism in the so-called American Dream. We must contest the notion that this dream is simply about giving every individual permission to engage in competitive races to the top.

At its best, sharing an identity as a people entails recognizing and honoring our *shared humanity* and our inherently social nature. It is about deeply held commitments to one another as fellow creatures—not pretending that differences do not matter (race, gender, sexual orientation, or class-blindness) and not reductionist view of others as *simply* ethnic, class, sexual, or racial groups, that is, alien strangers with whom we have nothing in common. (And it is certainly *not* about the current claim that "corporations" are people, too.) The remedying of exclusions that have long contradicted our claim that all are created "equal," that all have been granted the inalienable rights of "life, liberty, and the pursuit of happiness," requires a shared commitment to one another. It requires the refusal of binary categories for "good guys and bad guys." It requires acknowledging that the well-being of each group is tied up with the well-being of the others—of the "least of these," as a prophetic figure once said. Linking the iconoclastic criticism with such a vision of our shared humanity also requires that we refuse to idolize the inhabitants/members of the nation called the United States of America. Our concern for the "other" requires a generosity for other geographical populations as well as our own, thus disrupting idolized national boundaries and the recognition that we can "receive" from the other—we can learn from the wisdom of those whose lives are very different from our own.

Yet even these two crucial values—the importance of iconoclastic self-criticism, especially for those with the most power, combined with a rereading of our identity as a people such that our well-being is inextricably bound up with the well-being of the "others"—do not guarantee a national identity that addresses the deep wounds of exclusion. Self-criticism in the name of *justice* must be lived out. Remember, these exclusions have been generated by deeply internalized images and habits of thought and action of the "other." Important as it is, for example, to recognize our "whiteness," if we have racial dominance, or to accept an enhanced image of our corporate belonging, the visceral and pre-reflective character of aversion requires something other than *ideas* about how to fix things. "Redeeming" such exclusions requires contexts that flesh out and habituate us into new forms of "seeing" and experiencing those who are "other," including those our society has designated as worthless with no contribution to make to society. And this may be the biggest challenge of all, especially considering the variously distributed modes of power and othering.

While legal exclusions are gone, residual and new forms of "segregation" still prevent us from face-to-face relationships that might alter our experience of those who are different from us. Markers of privilege still tend to correlate with homogeneous neighborhoods, religious communities, and social networks. Talk about welcoming the other rarely coincides with face-to-face relationships that might enhance that change as a real possibility. The contexts of most Christian churches, for example, where the language of inclusion and welcome combine with face-to-face relations continue to reproduce class, race, and other forms of homogeneity, and the "other" is only present as a liturgical phrase.

What we need are not relations that continue our stratifications of class, race, gender, or so-called abilities, but relations where the discourse and status are somehow equalized and honest conversations can begin. I close with a couple of examples. With regard to so-called race differences, we need contexts not only where the "colorblind population" can come to recognize that we have race ("whiteness"), acknowledge that privilege, and address our unacknowledged biases, but also where we experience people of color as of the same status and where people of color can help develop relationships with "whites" where they can be honest, and see us in new ways. While acknowledgement of white privilege is most typically found in dismantling racism trainings, these contexts do not provide regular long-lasting community relationships. Interracial and multiethnic churches, which at least offer the opportunity for regular long-lasting "community," do not always offer the honest dialogues about privilege and bias that happen in the explicit trainings (Edwards 2008; Fulkerson, 2007). So both contexts have crucial practices to offer.

Some forms of oppressive gender relations remind us that it would be a mistake to romanticize all face-to-face relational contexts, insofar as they can reproduce hierarchical-submissive relations that can cover up domestic violence. However, ongoing face-to-face relationships can sometimes alter the dynamics of charity. This can happen when persons with ostensible power and agency—those of us considered "normal," for example, place ourselves in contexts where we must learn from the other, an "other" typically stereotyped as without agency. L'Arche, founded by

Jean Vanier, is just such a community where people with and without so-called disabilities live together, providing a setting where the "normate" learn new forms of agency and value that the larger culture has typically disdained. Whatever it takes, however, "life, liberty, and the pursuit of happiness" requires settings where both can "humanize" the other and disrupt dominant stereotypical images. We must be affectively habituated into honoring the other—whatever that will take.

Conclusion

My account of "American values" invites reinterpretations that will not be bought into by all. Reading "under God" as an imperative to self-criticism *rather than* a call to "Christianize" the nation will not be an easy sell for some. The radical honoring of all, especially those we experience as alien to our own identities, challenges the notion that those in power earned it and deserve it; those without power are lazy bums. The claim that we all have a stake in one another's life and well-being is a direct *counter* to the view that our life and liberty should be about freedom to pursue individualistic "happiness." I also commend practices that alter affective and embodied habituations if we are to move beyond the injustices attached to "othering," *rather than* trust that our correct ideas about such matters will fix things.

We must honor truth, rejecting these false myths as an inadequate version of life, liberty, and the pursuit of happiness. Alternative robust enactments of these American values, including the necessary recovery of historical memory in its fullness, might move us toward engagement in the painful but crucial practices that truly liberate life for subordinated groups and, in less obvious ways, expand the happiness of dominant groups. Redeeming the deeply wounded American legacy of equality is not about reproducing a religion, even if some traditions, radically revised, can be vital to the process for those in faith communities. It is about radical generosity, hospitality and unending risk with one another.

References

Alcoff, Linda Martin. 2011. "Latinos Beyond the Binary." In *Decolonizing Epistemologies*, edited by Ada María Isasi-Díaz and Eduardo Mendieta. New York: Fordham. Available at www.alcoff.com/content/beyondbinary.html.

Azaransky, Sarah. 2011. *The Dream is Freedom: Pauli Murray and American Democratic Faith*. New York: Oxford University Press.

Bonilla-Silva, Eduardo. 2010. *Racism Without Racists: Color-Blind Racisms and the Persistence of Racial Inequality in the United States.* New York: Oxford University Press. Available at Crossroadsantiracism.org.

Edwards, Korie L. 2008. *The Elusive Dream: The Power of Race in Interracial Churches.* New York: Oxford University Press.

Emerson, Michael and George Yancey. 2011. *Transcending Racial Barriers: Towards a Mutual Obligations Approach.* New York: Oxford University Press.

Fulkerson, Mary McClintock. 2007. *Places of Redemption: Theology for a Worldly Church.* Oxford: Oxford University Press.

Institute for Dismantling Racism. Available at idrnc.org.

L'Arche USA. Available at larcheusa.org.

Padilla, Laura M. 2001. "'A Dirty Mexican': Internalized Oppression, Latinos & Law." *Texas Hispanic Journal of Law and Policy* 7: 61–113.

CHAPTER 11

The Political Divide

Stephanie Y. Mitchem

The rancorous partisan political divide provides a glimpse at two of the strands within American society. This divide is described often as progressive against the conservative, or something similar. Usually, the descriptions are only considered from either a political or a religious view. For this essay, I am going to blend the two, touching on how the political divide is also profoundly religious. On the one hand, there are religious conservatives who have worked to construct the United States into the Christian nation that they alone define. On the other, activists work to create greater equity around the world, informed by ethical and religious values that they infuse into political values.

Some Christian conservatives are fueled by their own dogmatic beliefs. They believe that passing these ideas on to the nation through politics is a calling. Passing on their ideas is too often by means of political power and people control. The team sports' rules of coaches and star players using defensive and offensive moves become strategies to promote ideas in the American political landscape. In this form, there are always leaders and followers, always winners and losers. The single player only collaborates with his or her own team; everybody else is an "Other."

Such a team sports approach used by Charles Colson (1931–2012). Colson had worked for President Nixon and, after the scandal of Watergate, served some months in prison for obstruction of justice in the mid-1970s. Becoming a radical Christian, Colson began a Prison Fellowship after serving his time and began other organizations to promote his version of Christianity and America. With this version in mind, Colson built a team, its guiding principles outlined in a 1994 essay *First Things* (Colson 1994). He built the team with like-minded evangelical and Catholic Christians, stating that "Christians individually and the church corporately also have a responsibility for the right ordering of civil society." (Colson 1994) The list of the document's signatories included notable leaders of the Southern Baptist Convention, Assemblies of God, and other evangelical groups. The list of Catholics signatories included Catholic theologians, several bishops, and a cardinal. Mixing selected biblical quotations, papal instructions, and a heavy dose of Americana language, Colson managed to put the signatories into bed with the country's founders: "With them, we hold that only a virtuous people can be free and just, and that virtue is secured by religion" (Colson 1994).

Even while waving an American flag of freedom and virtue under religion, a qualification was constructed:

> Alone among world cultures, however, the West has cultivated an attitude of self-criticism and of eagerness to learn from other cultures. What is called multiculturalism can mean respectful attention to human differences. More commonly today, however, multiculturalism means affirming all cultures but our own. Welcoming the contributions of other cultures and being ever alert to the limitations of our own, we receive Western culture as our legacy and embrace it as our task in order to transmit it as a gift to future. (Colson 1994)

The "West" is a chilling mantra used by many Christian conservatives pointing to the rightness of a white world that exists in their white imaginations about a world before the 1960s social movements. People of color and women are often seen as destructive forces weakening the fabric of society. With clearly defined insider/outsider lines drawn, the religious community, by Colson's measure, can become a time capsule in whiteness, Western thought, and cultural suppression.

In order to widely affect the American landscape, their vision must be turned into law. "We strongly affirm the separation of church and state, and just as strongly protest the distortion of that principle to mean the separation of religion from public life." Colson clearly promotes theocracy, that is, a nation's rule by one religion's (read: evangelical Christianity's) leaders.

This envisioned Christian nation ignores a history of imperialism and thinks in terms of becoming a contemporary empire leading the world. Colson and his group stated: "We are profoundly aware that the American experiment has been, all in all, a blessing to the world and a blessing to us as Evangelical and Catholic Christians. We are determined to assume our full share of responsibility for this 'one nation under God'" (Colson 1994). This domination begins with control of the membership and then reaches across multiple playing fields.

The first step is obedience and control of the members. Theological legerdemain is needed to create an effective doctrine of obedience. Fear and guilt are writ large in such approaches to member control. There are several gruesome television advertisements for a particular ministry, one showing an operating room as the patient is flatlining. The medical staff work frantically to save the person and the minister stands as commentator outside the scene: "You will DIE! Are YOU ready to meet GOD??!!" Such approaches create a God who is to be feared at all times. The members then have a mortal dread of stepping outside the box created by the doctrines of some pastoral person. Therefore, I was not surprised when a faithful church member refused to go to a yoga class because her pastor instructed her that "Yoga is from the devil."

In like manner, stressing rules about the sexuality, sexual practices, birth and marriage plans of the congregation are somewhat safe areas for dogma and doctrine. The antiabortion fervor of conservative Christians becomes part of the wider tableau on sexuality control. Feminism, in itself, could be considered evil in this world because it makes women think bad thoughts, bring lawsuits, and change the proper structure of the world.

Of course, anything that falls outside heteronormativity can be identified as resulting from systemic evils like bad legislation, evil courts, wild feminists, gay marriage, and so on. The "proper" roles of women and men become control sticks that congregations can wield. Terrible guilt can result when a member thinks about sex or sexuality differently than the congregation demands—a lot of that guilt hides in closets of brothels and rest stops. But this emphasis on sex also means that there is no time for members to think about their churches' stands on war, peace, economic injustice, health, and so on. There is no room to self-analyze regarding actions toward others—"I tithe" is the new personal absolution for action against poverty, hunger, illness, strangers, and immigrants. Social justice items are reduced to prayer without teeth: "God, please help all the poor, hungry people." In prayer without action, the divine is reduced to a magical being. Sin is reduced to a little box of "me" and never understood as having a societal dimension.

The current state of politics that could be seen in the 2012 presidential elections offered some terrifying snapshots of many Americans, such as during the debates that occurred among Republican candidates in 2011. Consider a crowd cheering Rick Perry's record of public executions during his term as governor. The spontaneous outburst of applause from the audience coupled with Perry's smug pride in over 200 executions smacked of a mob mentality. Some statements evoke sharp irony in their cruelty. Many Americans believe that the anger expressed in such statements springs from racism toward a Black President Obama. And so irony enters the picture. The accusations of President Obama's health-care plan being an effort to "kill grandma" while wholesale death is promoted by those who rabidly resist anything the president might propose, indicates that something is severely wrong.

Therefore, with this kind of political-religious leadership, profound confusion about the ends of society and the meaning of community cause moral whiplash. Yes, we should be responsible for self. No, we should not help the poor. Yes, we should be compassionate. No, there should be no entitlements. Yes, corporations are people. No, people should not become members of unions. Yes, we need to educate the young. No, we should not pay teachers much. Hate speech may be illegal but the language of hatred has become so sophisticated that the number of disenfranchised, numb, apathetic people increases.

There is a political vision in the religious views espoused by Colson and his ilk: individual rights always take precedence over community. Personal responsibility is more important than community. Communism, socialism, and communes are to be feared in their world because individual rights are supplanted by the will of the group. Among the flaws in their perspectives: the dream society becomes a system that supersedes human volition, the very prize they guard. Those people who do not obey the call to individualism, even if physically or mentally incapable, are left by the side of the road. In this political vision, the supremacy of human will with an individualistic focus is compounded with a denial of community, therefore, becoming a brutal, nasty fulfillment of a Hobbesian society.

President Barack Obama addressed the British Parliament on May 25, 2011 and stated: "Repression offers only the false promise of stability." That has been the false promise of the Colson group and other social controllers. Eventually, humans stop cooperating with dictators. I once asked a famous feminist theologian how she came to be a feminist theologian. She was one of the first, trained in classical (read inherently misogynist) Christian thought. She paused for a moment. "Well, the men thought we were stupid."

In like manner, those who would engineer American society into their own image and likeness do not recognize that humans think. Thinking is the bane of dictators. Many people, across generations, recognize levels of hypocrisy in religious talk: advocating the right to life while cheering public executions; the expected "submissive" role of women in some denominations; the promotion of carrying guns as a human right while same-sex relationships are not. Some years ago, theologians and pastors decried what they termed "cafeteria" Christianity. More recently, pastors anguish over people making statements like "I'm spiritual, not religious." Spirituality, however, is a facet of being human. People are not stupid and will look to all sorts of places to find answers. The power of religions may be less than the religious or political leaders think. Fear has its limits. Or, as it was stated: "Repression offers only the false promise of stability."

This is where the other side of the political divide enters. Something has begun with the Occupy Wall Street, or Occupy Together Movement. On the Occupy Together web pages, a statement challenges the narrow views of the world while recognizing human connectivity.

> Global civil society is being threatened by a system based on power and not on human values. Day after day it represses basic freedoms and consistently favors the greed of the few over the needs of the many. This power finances wars, food and pharmaceutical monopolies, it sponsors dictatorial regimes across the globe, destroying environments, manipulating and censoring information flow and transparency. Despite our different cultural backgrounds and social contexts, we all suffer the same threats. Our freedom and dignity are under attack as a result of market dynamics and corrupt government institutions that are turning our local and global societies into increasingly unjust places. The governments of this planet must work for the people, not against them (occupytogether.org).

In comparison with a Colson type of group, there is a much different moral vision embedded in this statement. This statement is not explicitly religious, which may bother some religious people. Yet, it is a statement that is comfortable in a national or global setting. The United States promotes the idea of religious freedom, which goes back to nation's founding. This freedom is not really clear and often falls into myth and the term is subject to wide ranging interpretations. There are at least two different ways to think about religious freedom: freedom of religion or freedom for religion. Freedom OF religion promotes religious diversity. Freedom for religion promotes lobbying activities. Separation of church and state furthers freedom of religion. Theocracy promotes freedom for religion.

People continue to think and question and that is clear from the quotation in that governments, the author contends, must work for the people. As such, community is built and radical individualism is not valued. The excerpt presents a different view of power as power with rather than power over. Both of these are ideas that most religions can support. There is a currency to these words that speaks in other national contexts. If control is the byword of the Colson vision, this excerpt would speak of cooperation.

The Occupy Wall Street protests that began in September 2011 have spread throughout the United States and the globe with protests happening in places I would never have imagined them happening, like Spartanburg, South Carolina. Wall Street bankers are not impressed: "Some on Wall Street viewed the protesters with disdain and a degree of caution... Others say they feel their pain, but are befuddled about they are supposed to do to ease it. A few even feel personally attacked... Generally, bankers dismiss the protesters as gullible and unsophisticated." (Schwarts and Dash 2011). One reason that the Occupy protesters are considered gullible is that they have no identifiable leader; this is a problem for those who understand power as power over. The Occupy protesters also are willing to work in order to build consensus, another problem for those who take a hierarchical approach. Like the Arab Spring and the resistance to those in power.

However, the Occupy protesters are not the first in the modern era to rethink relationships between power and people. In December 1948, the Universal Declaration of Human Rights was adopted by the United Nations as a response to the inhumanity of World War II (http://www.un.org/en/documents/udhr/history.shtml). That declaration reset the framework by which we can understand human relationships and global cooperation. The first Article states: "All human beings are born free and equal in dignity and rights. They are endowed with reason and conscience and should act towards one another in a spirit of brotherhood." (http://www.un.org/en/documents/udhr/) Within that framework, a focus on religion comprises one of the articles of the declaration:

Article 18: Everyone has the right to freedom of thought, conscience and religion; this right includes freedom to change his religion or belief, and freedom, either alone or in community with others and in public or private, to manifest his religion or belief in teaching, practice, worship and observance.

Over 50 years later, the Occupy Together Movement brings the UN Universal Declaration on Human Rights from theory to practice. Human rights is not abstract but material and concrete. The dimensions of religious belief need to be enacted as praxis as well, to become liberatory across the political spectrum.

The feelings about connecting religious ideas to practices are also not new. Daniel Dennett spoke of this longing in January 2010.

> I look forward to the day when violence done under the influence of religious passion is considered more dishonorable, more shameful, than crimes of avarice, and is punished accordingly, and religious leaders who incite such acts are regarded with the same contempt that we reserve for bartenders who send dangerously disabled people out onto the highways.... The double standard that exempts religious activities from almost all standards of accountability should be dismantled once and for all.... Religious leaders and apologists should accept that since their institutions are so influential in American life, we have the right to hold their every move up to the light. (Dennett 2010)

This is passion. The need to connect praxis and theory, to connect religion and politics in ways that are real, this is the motivation for many to find Colson repulsive and the Occupy Movement admirable.

The Colson Center for Christian Worldview continues the vision of its founder. As their website reflects on results of the 2012 elections, the definition of the political divide as "holy" is also a call to keep it up: "2012 also divided our society in striking ways. The world didn't quite end, but the battles over the sanctity of life, over redefining marriage, and over religious freedom reached new levels and saw bold lines drawn in the sand by Christians unwilling to surrender what Christ claims for His own" (www.colsoncenter.org/issues/themeoftheweek/entry/42/21157).

At the same time, the Occupy Movement has also begun to use the religious theme of Jubilee: "Jubilee comes from many faith traditions including Judaism, Christianity, and Islam. A jubilee is an event in which all debts are cancelled and all those in bondage are set free." The new Occupy effort is called Rolling Jubilee and it raises funds to buy consumer and mortgage debt from banks and then cancels them, a new activist way to resist debt, to redefine power (rollingjubilee.org).

The religious dimensions of the political divide are clearer. The next years will bring new stories and new expressions of these divergent meaning worlds.

References

Charles Colson Center for Christian Worldview. Available at http://www.joincolson.com/become-a-member.php?utm_source=Google_Chuck&utm_medium=cpc&utm_content=AD2&utm_campaign=2011_Brand&gclid=CPvFwJ-jzawCFYHe4AodTmwyrg. Accessed November 23, 2011.

Colson, Charles. 1994. "Evangelicals & Catholics Together: The Christian Mission in the Third Millennium." *First Things*. Available at http://www.firstthings.com/article/2007/01/evangelicals – catholics-together-the-christian-mission-in-the-third-millennium-2. Accessed September 2011.

Dennett, Daniel C. 2010. "Religious No Longer a Protected Class." *The Washington Post*. "On Faith" blog, January 12. Available at http://newsweek.washingtonpost.com/onfaith/panelists/daniel_c_dennett/2010/01/religious_no_longer_a_protected_class.html. Accessed January 17, 2010.

Occupy Together. Available at http://www.occupytogether.org/. Accessed November 23, 2011.

Schwarts, Nelson D. and Eric Dash. 2011. "In Private, Wall St. Bankers Dismiss Protesters as Unsophisticated." *The New York Times*, October 15, B1.

Universal Declaration of Human Rights. Available at http://www.un.org/en/documents/udhr/history.shtml. Accessed November 23, 2011.

CHAPTER 12

Revitalizing US Civil Society by Reconceptualizing Civil Religion and Its Virtues

Rosemary P. Carbine

U
S civil society is arguably in decline if not effectively endangered. Civil society refers to a shared associational and discursive space of political inquiry, deliberation, and decision making among all citizens with different viewpoints about pressing issues that confront our common life and that connect to the common good. According to theologians and ethicists such as David Tracy, Francis Fiorenza, Jeffrey Stout, and Rebecca Chopp (Carbine 2006), practices that foster civil society in an increasingly pluralistic global setting are intertwined with civic virtues of mutual respect for the life, liberty, and equality of others, especially religious others. These virtues ground and emerge from the giving and exchanging of arguments, listening to and speaking with others in publicly accessible ways that recognize but bridge religious differences, and a willingness to consent to, dissent from, and/or risk a changed opinion about matters of common concern. By contrast, judging from recent political trends, US political discourse and public life are currently fractured, marked by a culture of labels and lies, which eviscerates civil society and its virtues.

In both the 2008 and 2012 US presidential campaigns, the relentless stereotyping of President Barack Obama as a terrorist, big business ally, socialist, communist, atheist, Muslim, Hindu, non-US citizen, and in other ways "foreign" signifies increasing racial and other forms of stratification, polarization, and fragmentation in US public life (Cunnigen and Bruce, eds. 2010; Espinosa, ed. 2011, chapters 9 and 11; Harvey Wingfield and Feagin 2010; Obama 2006, chapter 7). Similar to the billboard in Grand Junction, Colorado in fall 2010 that depicted Obama as a terrorist, gangster, Mexican bandit, and gay man, caricatures of Obama persist in the face of demonstrable facts about his US citizenship, his Christian identity, his disinterest in national-izing banks, and so on. *Newsweek* polls in September 2010 showed that portraying Obama as a threatening outsider (by trading on symbolic representations of "others") has gained popular traction. Twenty-four percent of Americans consider Obama a Muslim (an increase from 13 percent in 2008), 31 percent think Obama sympathizes with imple-menting fundamentalist Islamic law, and 50 percent question Obama's antiterrorism policies as weak. Putting this political smearing strategy into historical perspective, journalist Jonathan Alter posited that "grow-ing numbers of Americans think the president is a Muslim [because] more and more voters don't like him personally, and so are increasingly ready to believe anything critical (and to them being Muslim is a nega-tive) about someone they are already inclined to resent" (Alter 2010). Indeed, the birther movement, which contested Obama's birthplace and citizenship, decreased the electorate's tendency to identify Obama as Muslim to 11 percent, according to more recent Gallup polls, but increased the electorate's uncertainty about his identity to 44 percent (Landsberg 2012).

Significant blocs of the American electorate have channeled this personal dislike, religious resentment, and generalized xenophobia into anger-based voting. Before the US congressional midterm elections in fall 2010, *Newsweek* polls mapped this angry electorate: 23 percent of voters self-described as angry; the majority identified as conservative (Republican, Independent, Tea Party), and the majority vented political anger at existing congressional leaders. Angry voters begat angry candi-dates. The same *Newsweek* polls showed that 74 percent of angry voters supported a candidate angry about the economy and jobs, 75 percent backed a candidate angry about the federal budget, and 66 percent con-sidered Obama either insufficiently angry or too detached from real-life concerns. Interpreting these polls, anger mixed with anti-intellectual-ism now play a major role in the US political process and public life. Recent studies in political psychology by Drew Westen and George Lakoff conclude that voters stubbornly hold emotionally based convic-tions despite contradictory, evidence-based information (Begley 2010). Taking these political trends as an illustrative index of the present US political climate, the United States apparently cannot sustain civil society-based practices and virtues for dialogue, for reasonable debate, and for disagreements about common concerns without demonization and without nationwide threats of secession that appeared after the 2012 election (Fernandez 2012, 2013).

In the wake of impoverished genuine civic interchange about our pressing common concerns, some US political movements and actors promote the revitalization of civil society by returning to and rethinking American civil religion. Coined by sociologist Robert Bellah (Bellah 1970), civil religion refers to a shared political religion of commonly held sacred symbols (the flag, the Liberty Bell), sites (prominent political figures' memorials on the National Mall in Washington, DC), texts (the Declaration of Independence, the US Constitution), and practices (reciting the pledge of allegiance, celebrating national holidays) that create a national identity among America's diverse citizenry. Many of these symbols, sites, texts, and practices are indelibly imprinted with the historical legacies of manifest destiny, or allegedly divinely ordained US expansion and colonialism exemplified in the conquest of First Nation peoples, the annexation of the southwest after the Mexican-American War, and the acquisition of the Philippines, Cuba, and Puerto Rico after the Spanish-American War; of racism, sexism, and other prejudices enshrined in the US Constitution and continually "corrected" with the 13th, 14th, 15th, 19th, 24th, and 26th Amendments after the struggles of wars and social movements; and, of US exceptionalism and triumphalism found in increased flag-waving patriotism after the 9–11 al-Qaeda attacks and again after the assassination of Osama bin Laden in May 2011. Nevertheless, drinking deeply from the wells of America's civil religion found in democratic traditions may well stimulate a search for a moral compass that better promotes civil society–based practices and virtues, such as the inalienable rights to life, liberty, and the pursuit of happiness in the Declaration of Independence that are linked with justice and the general welfare in the US Constitution. In other words, reconceptualizing our shared religio-political traditions of life, liberty, and happiness—in relation to justice and the common good—opens up the possibility of renewing US public life itself. Assessing these traditions is needed, given the growing ideological, regional, and political partisan divides about liberty in the United States—from voting to women's health issues—during and after the 2012 presidential election (Blow 2012).

This essay critically compares emerging and operative religio-political notions of civil religion in US conservative and liberal political camps in order to explore what each camp envisions as politically possible for the common good, that is, as an alternative possible world that offsets the fractured civil society in which we currently live, and move, and have our being in the United States, politically speaking. In keeping with E. J. Dionne's analysis in *Souled Out*, this essay examines the ways in which conservative camps claim to preserve and restore US democratic traditions whereas liberal camps contextualize and clarify those same traditions for new eras, traditions such as sacred texts and central moral values that provide religio-political underpinnings for the public good (Dionne 2008, 28–29; see also Hunter 2010; Shields 2009; Shiffrin 2012). Drawing on Glenn Beck's Restoring Honor Rally and the PBS-sponsored By The People events,[1] this essay analyzes these camps' competing views of American civil religion rooted either in particular Christian or in more humanistic civic virtues, which consequently fuel contrasting notions of the common good. Gaining a better understanding of each camp's approach to civil religion will illustrate each camp's practices for regenerating civil society and its associated virtues with the goal to revive our shared life together.

Conservatives: Restoring Civil Religion via Christian Virtues

On Saturday, August 28, 2010 in Washington, DC, between 100–500,000 people packed the National Mall between the Lincoln Memorial and the Washington Monument to participate in the Restoring Honor Rally sponsored by Glenn Beck. Considered a charismatic leader and educator in a resurgent conservative Christian movement after the decline of the Religious Right, Beck promoted this rally via his daily radio show and (now defunct) television program. Beck is renowned for his religiously based end-times or rapture politics and chalkboard conspiracy theories. After discovering the "coincidence" between the rally's date and the anniversary of the March on Washington for Jobs and Freedom, Beck proposed to reclaim and reinvent this iconic moment in the US Civil Rights Movement for a conservative agenda via this rally. (Beck's claim contradicted his strident criticism of US Protestant, Catholic, Latino, and African American churches for preaching social justice, which he equated with Communist and Nazi code words.) Drawing much criticism for this comparison,[2] Beck billed the rally not as a civil rights or even a political event, but as a "salute to the troops" and "world changing event" to unveil "The Plan," a divinely inspired set of principles and practices to refound America.

In my view, the nearly four-hour-long rally resembled a repentant return to apparently lost American values and virtues, which Beck and others regard as a pivot point established by America's founders and upheld by present-day American military veterans as well as exemplary citizens. After the rally opened with the pledge of allegiance and the national anthem, Beck introduced the event in religious revivalesque terms: "America today begins to turn back to God." Pastor D. Paul Jehle, a descendant from Mayflower Pilgrims, called the crowd in the invocation to repent from inequalities, from broken covenants with Native American peoples, from abortion and same-sex marriage, and instead to seek reconciliation as one nation under God. Rather than political placards, Tea Party and other conservative activists at the rally intertwined piety and patriotism by carrying crosses, Bibles, and flags, thereby using these symbols to (albeit falsely) foster their "America is a Christian nation" origins story. About midway through the rally, Dr. Alveda King, niece of Martin Luther King Jr., led the crowd in a Black church-style service that incorporated biblical readings and gospel music–inspired hymns centered on racial and religious unity under God, more specifically under Christ. King's sermon closed the service with this "dream": "I have a dream that one day soon God's adoptive love will transcend skin color and economic status and cause us to turn from moral turpitude.... [and] receive everyone as brothers and sisters in the love of God."

Continuing to pair Christian piety and US patriotism in a way that verged on Christian theocratic nationalism, the rally participated in a politics of national memory because it took place amid sacred sites and spaces of American civil religion, surrounded by its major figures and texts. In his opening remarks, Beck referred reverently to the "noble" Washington Monument and its inscription "praise be to God," described the Jefferson Memorial as a "monument to liberty," to God-given liberty and justice for all, and portrayed the Lincoln Memorial as a "temple of freedom" dedicated to equality and charity, with Lincoln seated on its "throne of authority." Beck treated and interpreted the Declaration of Independence, the US Constitution, several of Lincoln's addresses, and other documents as "American scripture." Taking a cue from the Mall's reflecting pool and drawing a lesson from this political trinity of American leaders, Beck identified three civic virtues that framed the event: "With charity to those who struggle, faith in a God that loves and guides us, and hope in the truth of who we really are, we begin today to pledge to restore...America."

Former Republican vice-presidential nominee, evangelical godly woman, and popularly canonized "saint" Sarah Palin (Miller 2010; Griffith 2011) expanded this list of virtues when she presented a George Washington–instituted badge of merit to military veterans. Beyond faith, hope, and charity, Palin added courage in the face of impossible odds, a quest for justice and mercy (found in the Sermon on the Mount), and patriotism. Following Palin, Beck awarded this same merit badge to ordinary citizens who exemplified these virtues—an African American Baptist pastor who founded many churches in the Houston, Texas area, a Latino baseball player involved in evangelization ministries and in a Down's syndrome foundation, and a billionaire philanthropist who created a cancer research institute. In Beck's view, these virtues served as "the cornerstone of America's foundation," and recalled a time when "this faith that once guided us"—aka Christianity—made America "an eternal flame," paralleling both the Puritan's and President Reagan's religio-political vision of the United States as a city on a hill for the world to emulate.

Beck stated in his signature speech at the rally that "this day has nothing to do with politics; it has everything to do with God, with turning our face back to the values and principles that made us great." In that speech, Beck invoked Christian seasons of ascetic discipline or personal preparation before definitive holy days, such as Advent and Lent, and called the crowd to "go to God boot camp." He urged them to repeat the 40 Day / 40 Night challenge issued prior to the rally and thereby renew their personal faith, hope, and charity. Offering a literal and moral exegesis of American sacred scriptures, Beck articulated guiding civic commandments drawn from the conclusion of the Declaration of Independence: "With a firm reliance on the protection of Divine Providence, we mutually pledge to each other our Lives, our Fortunes, and our sacred Honor." Beck directed the crowd to reaffirm belief in God and in humanity as God's children, pledge their lives (at personal sacrifice) to one other, to their communities and to future generations, and practice tithing as well as truth-telling. Returning to a rapture-based politics, Beck endorsed these commandments and practices in order to prepare America for weathering an approaching apocalyptic storm.[3]

A new term aptly characterizes a Christian conservative approach to American civil religion and civil society manifested in Beck's rally—"Republicanity." Some of the religio-political features of Republicanity include *mythologies* of American origins focused on the Christianity of the founders and of founding documents, *rituals* such as rallies or pledges that reflect defining concerns and commitments, *ethical teachings* and moral guidelines drawn from American sacred texts to preserve and protect "the American way," and *fundamentalist theologies of divine providence* in anointing political leaders or plans (Laderman 2011). Taking a closer look at Beck's rally through the lens of the mythology and mores of Republicanity's civil religion sheds new light on a Christian conservative approach to renewing US civil society.

With regard to mythology, Restoring Honor captures the increasing popularity of a "return to the founders" rhetoric in which political elites retell America's origins story of foundational figures and sacred scriptures in a religiously and historically revisionist way. 2012 Republican presidential contender Rep. Michele Bachmann created a Congressional Tea Party Caucus that held weekly seminars to educate about Christianity's influence on America's founders and constitutional history. Moreover, Republicans inaugurated the 112th Congress in January 2011 by reading aloud the most updated version of the US Constitution, which oversimplified and invisibilized many contentious debates that shaped both the original version and its later amendments. What these conservative constitutional activists overlook is the lack of any overtly religious (specifically Christian) origins or inspiration in the US Constitution. By contrast, the founders' Enlightenment rationalist and Deist beliefs in a nontrinitarian, nonprovidential Creator radically oppose Republicanity's mythos that equates America with a Christian nation (Maier 1998, 2010; Romano 2010; Schama 2011). Nonetheless, this romanticized US origins story and its false Christian nation mythology revive US civil society for some conservatives by fusing religion not only with politics and government, but also with family, education, the arts, media, and business in order to craft a Christian dominant world, or what is called Christian Dominionism (Goldberg 2006; Ingersoll 2009; Lizza 2011).

With regard to mores, restoring America at Beck's rally depended on instilling Christianity's theological virtues—faith, hope, and love—in individuals, and by doing so regain a perceived-to-be-lost prominent place for Christianity in US civil society. Beck repeatedly charged the crowd to stand at a symbolic crossroads and cultivate individual morality, to become "individuals of faith, individuals of hope, individuals of charity." This focus on individual virtue underscores Beck's restorationist or protectionist political theology, which preserves a perceived predominant Christian status quo rather than imagines another alternative possible public realm. Rather than commend these virtues for life in an increasingly pluralistic global society, Beck ended the rally by introducing 240 Christian, Jewish, and Muslim leaders committed to conservative constitutional activism—to "protect sacred scriptures and texts of our country and of our faith," albeit an implied shared faith across these monotheistic traditions.

Based on an informal ethnographic study of the rally, Alex McNeill echoed one of the speeches from an Iraq war veteran's mother, claiming "salvation for themselves and for the country is an individual act." Rather than trade self-interest for the greater common good, for our collective life, liberty, and pursuit of happiness tempered by justice and by the public weal, McNeill observed that the rally's "individualism is focused on personal attainment, personal happiness, and personal livelihood, and fails to see how each relies on a system that empowers, privileges, or dispossesses either the individual or others in the process.... [T]o shift the conversation from 'I' to 'we' in speaking of collective liberation was quickly flagged as anti-American and dismissed" (McNeill 2010). Rather than channel civic virtues for the public good, "we must not fundamentally transform America," as Sarah Palin argued, rather "we must restore America and restore her honor"—which begins and ends with individuals, and has little effect on embracing differences, healthy disagreements, and routes to consensus-building that are much needed for life in a thriving US civil society. Moreover, as demonstrated in the US budget debate in 2011–2012, this individualistic turn reflects an Ayn Rand–influenced view that prizes the freedom—especially of the wealthy—from a government that provides for the common good partly via a social safety net for the well-being of the less-wealthy (Chait 2011; Townsend 2011). Notwithstanding the top-down theocratic Christian God-talk in Republicanity's mythos of American origins, trickle-up religion and mores in and beyond Beck's rally stresses individual renewal with social implications for the elite, but ultimately bears little sociopolitical efficacy for altering the existing tenor and widening gaps within US society.

Liberals: Living Civil Religion via Civic Virtues

In 2002, MacNeil/Lehrer Productions together with the Rockefeller Brothers Fund, the Kellogg Foundation, the Center for Deliberative Democracy at Stanford University, and the Institution for Social and Policy Studies at Yale University launched a nonpartisan project titled "By The People" (BTP). BTP articulates its mission to "bring the views of informed, ordinary citizens to a national discussion on the important issues of the day." Since its founding, BTP has hosted approximately

200 events, called citizen deliberations, and over 100 broadcasts about various topics based on those events. Each event encouraged a randomly selected sample of diverse US citizens to participate in informed discussions with experts and with one another about locally and nationally significant issues. Attendees also took pre-event and post-event polls to gauge the efficacy of informed dialogue on their political opinions. Events utilized various formats, such as daylong or weekend-long dialogues, forums, panels, or roundtables at community colleges, and film screenings with talkbacks at libraries.

One of BTP's weekend-long dialogues invited 50 emerging and established US leaders from different professions and perspectives to discuss "Citizenship in the 21st Century" at Colonial Williamsburg, VA. Subtitled "Dialogues in Democracy: Life, Liberty and the Pursuit of Happiness," this fall 2007 event consisted of a three-day convocation with small group and plenary sessions that addressed US citizenship rights and responsibilities and culminated in the drafting of a modern-day Declaration of Citizenship. At the same time, nearly 1,100 US citizens assembled in 11 communities across 10 states to confer about a wide range of topics, including health care, education, immigration, housing, transportation, and the environment. This event, thus, epitomizes the revitalization of US civil society by returning to a sacred site in American civil religion, the House of Burgesses in Colonial Williamsburg "where the founding generation produced the first comprehensive Declaration of Rights," by placing those citizenship rights and responsibilities in both historical and contemporary contexts, and by doing so in a way that mobilized and enlivened a tradition of practical wisdom, of discursive strategies and dialogical virtues.

To redress what religion professor Barbara Brown Taylor, an attendee at the 2007 event, called "constitutional illiteracy," the attendees received background information to foster discussion about defining rights to life, liberty, and the pursuit of happiness. Some of those resources comprised the Declaration of Independence, the US Constitution, other documents from American sacred scriptures at the Colonial Williamsburg Foundation website, and a seven-page discussion guide that historically situated these nation-defining rights. The guide interpreted these rights as a moral guidepost both for the founders and for contemporary US citizens. The guide also listed questions for attendees to consider together about the meaning and exercise of these rights in an increasingly interconnected and globalized world. Questions focused on the basics of life and the role of government in maintaining and/or providing them; the protection of or limits on personal liberties in wartime;

and, the role of government in tackling economic, environmental, and other issues, such as abortion or same-sex marriage.

While invoking a "return to the founders" rhetoric, the guide treated the founders and founding rights not as a static, objective, or reified deposit of truths to be protected, cited, and used as proof texts to legitimate contemporary political attitudes and actions, but rather as a historical, contextual, and dynamic living tradition in need of reinvention in each era with creative fidelity. For example, the guide placed the right to life in past and present sociohistorical and economic contexts, noting that the founders lived in a mainly rural, agrarian society of 3 million, while the present US suburban/urban population of 300 million live in an increasingly technological world. The role of government in protecting life has thus fundamentally altered with the times, going beyond establishing a military for defense and peace to incorporating a wide array of social programs. In addition, liberty in the United States at its origins meant liberation from British colonial rule. At present, liberty "must be weighed," according to the guide, "against a backdrop of a post-9/11 world" and "a broad series of challenges," namely nuclear threats, terrorism, poverty, and religio-cultural strife, to name only a few. Furthermore, the US government originally promoted the pursuit of happiness economically by regulating trade, but the guide concluded with some pointed questions about the fundamental disconnect between crass materialist consumption of goods and the common good, noting that "drawing a distinction between a personal and public choice in today's diverse and globalized world is increasingly complex." Pursuing highly individualized happiness and practicing a "spectator" sort of citizenship only undermines the balance between individual rights and the responsibilities to protect others' rights.

Continuing to consider American sacred texts as a living, organic constitutional tradition, the event focused in its final task on drafting, debating, and revising a declaration of rights in modern-day America. History professor Carol Berkin reminded the attendees that the United States often refreshed its national identity by returning *both* to the democratic principles institutionalized by the founders *and* to ongoing struggles for better realizing those principles, whether in abolitionist, suffragist, civil rights, or other justice movements. Developed in small groups and then discussed in full plenary session, the resulting declaration listed rights in connection to ten contemporary issues—reproductive rights, civic engagement, the economy, education, the environment, health care, immigration, marriage and family, national security, and public information in a digital age. Significantly, about half of the declaration's statements stressed practicing civic virtues regardless of religious tradition. Also, the declaration linked virtues—such as responsibility, informed inquiry and participation, civility, civic education and engagement, moderation, mutual respect, and integrity—with a vibrant, sustainable democracy. Attendees used virtue as a moral term not to point to exemplars of these characteristics, but rather to denote and promote the obligations of all citizens to participate and engage in civic life—which the weekend modeled in itself. The event was filled with impassioned discourse and was framed by practical wisdom, that is, by a common commitment to civic virtues of the democratic process, such as equality and mutual goodwill across partisan and other differences, in order to avoid deeply polarized discourse and a divisive body politic. Nathan Baxter, an African American Episcopal bishop, captured these virtues in his comments: "This is perhaps the most important part of the democratic process, citizens really sitting down and sharing, listening to one another, and going through the whole process of moral suasion so that we can come to a more informed decision." And, Robyn Allen, a young white student, interrelated these virtues with treating American sacred scripture as a living tradition in relation to the weekend's task: "Even though we can't create something that will last for 100 or 200 years, I think we can give it our best shot and we can just say, 'Here's a cross-section of Americans. Here's what we've been thinking about for a few days.' And, hopefully this will spur discussion in the coming months and years."

In sum, the BTP citizen deliberation in 2007 reconceptualized US constitutional rights at the heart of American civil religion and in doing so the attendees embodied political skills and virtues of citizenship for reviving and sustaining civil society. Building on Jeffrey Stout's *Blessed Are the Organized*, this event modeled, in my view, grassroots democracy, in which participants understood "we, the people" not as an undifferentiated mass of utilitarian individuals who seek remedies for social problems that begin and end with the self, but rather as ordinary, politically organized, and responsible people (Stout 2010, 7, 230–231). For example, they exercised basic citizenship rights to assembly and to free speech, and they engaged in an informed, critically reflective exchange about common concerns in various formats—face-to-face conversations, small group meetings, and group action—to create a declaration of rights (Stout 2010, xvi, 56–57, 226–227). They practiced listening as "a democratic act" because their conversations undertook the work of citizenship—sharing stories about common concerns, and responding with empathy as well as with a view toward a more just society (Stout 2010, xvi, xviii). Moreover, they recognized that democracy subsists in relationships of mutual accountability for society, and thus held themselves and others accountable for sociopolitical contexts and conditions (Stout 2010, 10, 100, 117, 147). Finally, they expressed hope—disengaged from any specific religious tradition—in fashioning a new declaration of citizenship rights, which is, according to Stout, "the virtue one needs when grim facts might tempt one to give up on promoting or protecting important goods.... Democratic hope is a virtue that needs grounds.... grounds for thinking that we have a chance of making a significant difference for the better" (Stout 2010, 283). The resulting declaration of citizenship rights hardly acts as political leverage to shape public policy, although the statement on universal access to basic health care accords with the US Supreme Court ruling to uphold the Affordable Care Act, and the statement on marriage and family parallels district and appellate court rulings to overturn California's Proposition 8 that banned same-sex marriage. Nevertheless, the attendees articulated and acted on citizenship rights and responsibilities during their deliberations in ways that expressed and embodied those very same rights and responsibilities. Albeit in a fleeting way, they practiced skills and virtues for living in and into a renewed civil society (Stout 2010, 13).

Civil Society, Virtues, and Competing Conceptions of the Common Good

Interpreting some key political figures and events in US conservative and liberal camps from a theo-political perspective on civil religion has raised questions about how we shift in the United States from dysfunction to transformative civility, from capitulation to and desperation about the status quo to participation in humanizing conversations. Thus, this essay has highlighted each camp's means of restoring civil society through certain virtues in order to better identify and evaluate what each camp envisions as politically possible for the common good. Conservative camps illustrated by Beck's Restoring Honor rally offered an originalist sort of constitutionalist return to a Christian mythic and theocratic view of the common good, grounded in an individualist pursuit of the theological virtues of faith, hope, and charity. Liberal camps illustrated by the BTP's Dialogues in Democracy promoted a living constitutionalist tradition rooted in a grassroots democratic view of the common good and its associated civic virtues for dialogue—listening to, learning from, responding to, and respecting others from diverse and divergent contexts. Beyond a civil religion-based battle of constitutional hermeneutics between originalists and historicists, what conclusions can we draw from these rival visions of civil society, virtues, and views of common good?

Rather than define the common good only on negative terms as freedom from exclusion, domination, and other injustices (Stout 2010, 39, 41, 139–140, 247–248), we need to interpret the common good and its attendant political virtues in positive terms, or what Vatican II's "Pastoral Constitution on the Church in the Modern World" calls the collective conditions that enable and advance the full humanity and flourishing of all citizens, both individually and socially (Flannery 1996, 191–192). From this perspective, the common good resists an isolationist, individualist, or exclusivist group notion of political rights and responsibilities. Faith, hope, and charity are too easily privatized, individualized, and utilized to sacralize (or demonize) certain groups, which the Restoring Honor rally clearly demonstrated. What sorts of virtues, beyond the virtues for dialogue manifested in the BTP event, promote human fulfillment and flourishing, individually and collectively? After all, life thrives on more than talk. Former Georgetown University theology professor Monika K. Hellwig (d. 2005) surveyed in her last major work some political virtues—such as prudence (the correlation of means and ends), justice (fair and equal standards), fortitude (courage and endurance), and temperance (restraint)—as a theological framework for steering US society toward the common good (Hellwig 2005, 139–143). Practicing what the Christian tradition considers cardinal virtues and their correlative humanistic virtues may help us navigate through our often polarized public order and may also elicit other virtues that give us a glimpse of—but do not equal—the common good, virtues such as empathy and compassion for meeting human needs regardless of identity-markers, national borders, and partisan or religious interests (Hellwig, 88–89, 110–111). While framing a theological basis for the common good in a Christian perspective, these virtues may carry wider "common currency" or "moral capital" beyond specific political camps or religious traditions (Hellwig, 147). The BTP event contains some hallmarks for promoting this view of the common good and for finding that common currency. The BTP declaration of citizenship rights explicitly endorses empathy and compassion. In a non-militarist statement about the right to national security, for example, the declaration posits that "no citizen shall be abandoned to languish in conditions which threaten his or her survival, regardless of the circumstances that render the citizen in need." To better support life

in a pluralistic democracy, empathy and compassion rely on an inter-
dependent rather than individual commitment and practice in order to
achieve an idealistic goal: to enjoy and sustain a shared life together in a
pluralistic democracy that esteems dialogue—and much more.

Notes

1. Comedy Central talk show hosts Jon Stewart and Stephen Colbert cospon-
sored a satirical political counterpoint to Beck's rally, called the Rally to
Restore Sanity and/or Fear, on the National Mall in Washington, DC on
October 30, 2010. While exceeding Beck's rally in popularity, the Stewart-
Colbert rally did not offer an alternative kind of civic engagement that figures
centrally in this essay's analysis of the Right and the Left in US politics.
2. Historians have pointed out major political differences between the 1963
and the 2010 rallies. The former critically transformed US civil, political,
and economic rights in keeping with foundational US democratic principles
of liberty and equality. The latter uncritically upheld conservative, white,
middle-class, Christian America and its values, such as traditional heter-
onormative marriage and family, prayer in public places and schools, and
a strong military (Murphy 2010). Recent polls (Pew Forum 2011; Public
Religion 2010) also confirm the role of race in the Tea Party's fusion of social
and religious conservatism. White mainline and evangelical Protestants as
well as white Catholics identify and agree with the Tea Party's agenda that
backed Beck's rally.
3. Rep. Michele Bachmann interpreted the 5.8 magnitude earthquake and
Hurricane Irene that wreaked havoc on the East Coast in late August 2011
as a divine warning against Washington, DC. Also, between August 21
and 24, 2011, Beck hosted Restoring Courage, which culminated in a rally
in Jerusalem. The shift from gathering at America's seat of authority to
what Beck considers God's seat of authority involves, ostensibly, standing
with Israel in protest against the re-institution of the pre-1967 borders with
Palestine. In conservative Christian circles, this "symbolic destruction" of
Israel marks the start of an apocalyptic war between Israel and Gog-Magog
(Ezekiel 38–39; Revelation 20), a war that presages the *parousia* or Christ's
second coming.

References

Alter, Jonathan. 2010. "The Illustrated Man." *Newsweek*, September 6.
Beck, Glenn. 2010. "Make the Pledge—40 Days and 40 Nights." December 10.
  Available at www.glennbeck.com/content/articles/article/198/39452/#.
Begley, Sharon. 2010. "I'm Mad as Hell…and I'm Going to Vote!" *Newsweek*,
  October 11.

Bellah, Robert. 1970. "Civil Religion in America." In *Beyond Belief: Essays on Religion in a Post-Traditional World*, 168–186. New York: Harper and Row.

Blow, Charles M. 2012. "Lincoln, Liberty, and the Two Americas." *The New York Times*, November 23.

By The People. 2007. "Dialogues in Democracy: Life, Liberty and the Pursuit of Happiness in the 21st Century." November 8–11. Available at www.pbs.org/newshour/btp/projects/did.html and www.pbs.org/newshour/btp/projects/did2.html. For this event's discussion guide, see www.pbs.org/newshour/btp/files/HOB_backgrounder.pdf.

Carbine, Rosemary P. 2006. "Ekklesial Work: Toward a Feminist Public Theology." *Harvard Theological Review* 99.4: 433–455.

Chait, Jonathan. 2011. "War on the Weak." *Newsweek*, April 10.

Cunnigen, Donald and Marino A. Bruce, eds. 2010. *Race in the Age of Obama*. Bingley, UK: Emerald.

Dionne Jr., E. J. 2008. *Souled Out: Reclaiming Faith and Politics after the Religious Right*. Princeton and Oxford: Princeton University Press.

Espinosa, Gastón, ed. 2011. *Religion, Race, and the American Presidency*. Lanham, MD: Rowman and Littlefield.

Fernandez, Manny. 2013. "White House Rejects Petitions to Secede, But Texans Fight On." *The New York Times*, January 15.

———. 2012. "With Stickers, a Petition, and Even a Middle Name, Secession Fever Hits Texas." *The New York Times*, November 23.

Flannery, Austin. 1996. *Vatican Council II: The Basic Sixteen Documents: Constitutions, Decrees, Declarations*. Northport, NY: Costello Publishing.

Goldberg, Michelle. 2006. *Kingdom Coming: The Rise of Christian Nationalism*. New York: W. W. Norton.

Griffith, R. Marie. 2011. "The New Evangelical Feminism of Bachmann and Palin." *Huffington Post*, July 6.

Harvey Wingfield, Adia and Joe R. Feagin. 2010. *Yes We Can? White Racial Framing and the 2008 Presidential Campaign*. New York: Routledge.

Hellwig, Monika K. 2005. *Public Dimensions of a Believer's Life: Rediscovering the Cardinal Virtues*. Lanham, MD: Rowman and Littlefield.

Hunter, James Davison. 2010. *To Change the World: The Irony, Tragedy, and Possibility of Christianity in the Late Modern World*. New York and Oxford: Oxford University Press.

Ingersoll, Julie. 2009. "Mobilizing Evangelicals: Christian Reconstructionism and the Roots of the Religious Right." In *Evangelicals and Democracy in America: Religion and Politics*. Vol. 2, edited by Steven Brint and Jean Reith Schrodel, 179–208. New York: Russell Sage.

Laderman, Gary. 2011. "Republicanity—The GOP Transformation is Nearly Complete." *Religion Dispatches*, July 17.

Landsberg, Mitchell. 2012. "Poll: Most Americans Do Not Identify Obama as Christian." *Los Angeles Times*, June 23.

Lizza, Ryan. 2011. "Leap of Faith: The Making of a Republican Front-Runner." *The New Yorker*, August 15.

Maier, Pauline. 1998. *American Scripture: Making the Declaration of Independence.* New York: Random House.

Maier, Pauline. 2010. *Ratification: The People Debate the Constitution, 1787–1788.* New York: Simon & Schuster.

McNeill, Alex. 2010. "Me the People: A Day with the Tea Party." *Religion Dispatches*, August 30.

"Michele Bachmann's Hurricane Comments Were Only a Joke, She Says." 2011. *The Guardian*, August 30. Avai;lable at www.guardian.co.uk/world/2011/aug/30/michelle-bachmann-hurricane-warning-joke.

Miller, Lisa. 2010. "Saint Sarah." *Newsweek*, June 21.

Murphy, Andrew. 2010. "Beck Plays Prophet—Politics Pervade." *Religion Dispatches*, September 1.

Obama, Barack. 2006. *The Audacity of Hope: Thoughts on Reclaiming the American Dream.* New York: Three Rivers Press.

Pew Forum on Religion and Public Life. 2011. "The Tea Party and Religion." February 23. Available at http://pewforum.org/Politics-and-Elections/Tea-Party-and-Religion.aspx.

Public Religion Research Institute. 2010. "Survey: Religion and the Tea Party in the 2010 Elections." October 5. Available at www.publicreligion.org/research/published/?id=386.

Restoring Courage. August 24, 2011. Available at www.glennbeck.com/israel/

Restoring Honor. August 28, 2010. Available at www.glennbeck.com/content/articles/article/198/44980/ and www.c-spanvideo.org/program/295231–1.

Romano, Andrew. 2010. "America's Holy Writ." *Newsweek*, October 25.

Schama, Simon. 2011. "The Founding Fathers, Unzipped." *Newsweek*, July 4 and 11.

Shields, Jon A. 2009. *The Democratic Virtues of the Christian Right.* Princeton, NJ: Princeton University Press.

Shiffrin, Steven H. 2012. *The Religious Left and Church-State Relations.* Princeton, NJ: Princeton University Press.

Stout, Jeffrey. 2010. *Blessed Are the Organized: Grassroots Democracy in America.* Princeton, NJ and Oxford: Princeton University Press.

Townsend, Kathleen Kennedy. 2011. "Ayn Rand vs. America." *The Atlantic*, August 23.

CHAPTER 13

Latinas' and Latinos' Understanding of Life, Liberty, and the Pursuit of Happiness

Ada María Isasi-Díaz

Having arrived in the United States as a political refugee when I was 17 years old, I have lived most of my life keenly aware of the fact that I am considered an outsider by many I encounter every day and even by those I have worked with for decades. Very early on in my life, I felt obliged to learn about the movement of peoples across national borders and about the economics and politics of immigration.

Purposefully Unknown History

The United States is a nation of immigrants, of immigrants that violently displaced and mercilessly annihilated vast numbers of the indigenous people living here before their arrival. It was Ponce de Leon in 1513 who first claimed parts of this territory for Spain; but it was the French, fleeing Huguenots, who first established a small settlement in what is today Port Royal, South Carolina, and later established a colony at the mouth of the St. Johns River in Florida, in 1564. A year later Spain decided to eliminate the French settlement in Florida, claiming that this was a Spanish possession and because it considered the Huguenots as dangerous heretics. Both French and Spaniards slaughtered each other mercilessly; but the ones who lost the most were the indigenous people of the region. This happened 57 years before the arrival of *The Mayflower* at Plymouth Rock, Massachusetts.

At the other end of the territory of what today is the United States, took place the colonization by Spanish missionaries of California, and the annexation of Mexican territory (Texas) by the United States that led to the Mexican-American War (1846–1848). The peace treaty that ended this war obliged Mexico to cede all of its northern land, which included present-day California, Nevada, and Utah, as well as most of Arizona, New Mexico, and Colorado. This very brief historical account of a part of US history that is little known or remembered is an attempt to establish the historicity of the comings and goings of different peoples to the United States beyond the only one that seems to matter, that of the arrival of the Pilgrims in 1620.

Immigration in the Era of Globalization

Addressing migration in the twenty-first century requires understanding and placing this issue within the context of globalization, which is about the free flow of goods and capital, but mostly ignores the flow of people worldwide. Several features of globalization are contributing to displacement of people. Technological innovation and changes—mechanization, automation, computerization, and robotics—hugely increase productivity while decreasing the human labor needed to extract, produce, and distribute goods and many services. "Accelerated trade is replacing or undercutting domestic industrial and agricultural production with cheap imports, but at the expense of many jobs in those sectors." (Taran 2000) Today, therefore, migration is a closely tied to economic globalization, the epitome of neoliberal capitalism.

At the World Social Forum in Senegal, February 2011, I first learned about the different organizations working on this issue. Many of them advocate for the need to shift from national migration policies to an international one. If there is a General Agreement on Tariffs and Trade (GATT), and a General Agreement on Trade in Services (GATS), why can we not have a general agreement about the free international movement of people beneficial to the migrants, their countries of origin, and their countries of destination? Why not have a general agreement that accepts the free entry and exit of migrants? This is not an agreement easy to fashion, but the fact that nearly two hundred million persons are living outside their country of birth makes it necessary and of utmost importance. Migration is a global phenomenon and the "asymmetric macroeconomic incentives behind cross-border movements of people," urgently need a general agreement to "avoid brain drain effects in the emigration country and crowding out effects in the immigration area." (Straubhaar 2000, 9)

The other side of the coin of migration is the right of people not to migrate, to be able to stay in their countries of origin and find dignified work so they can earn what they need to provide for themselves and for those for whom they are responsible. A pastoral letter titled *Strangers No Longer* and written by Roman Catholic Mexican and US bishops in 2003 states it very clearly. "All persons have the right to find in their own countries the economic, political, and social opportunities to live in dignity and achieve a full life through the use of their God-given gifts. In this context, work that provides a just, living wage is a basic human need." The right not to migrate, then, demands national and international economic policies to respond to rights we all have, to live in dignity and support our loved ones without having to emigrate. As Catholic Relief Services recommended in 2003 during the negotiation of the Central American Free Trade Agreement, "The long-term goal is equitable development, with migration as a choice rather than a necessity."

Role of Immigrants in the United States

In a nation of immigrants like the United States, the realities of those who immigrate here cannot be ignored when redefining this country, as the present moment calls us to do. The reasons for people immigrating to the United States are an intrinsic element of the present social, political, and economic situation and, therefore, must be a central factor in any attempt to reinterpret the key values on which this country was founded: life, liberty, and the pursuit of happiness. The reason for this is *not only* because US economic and political policies are responsible for conditions in other countries from which people immigrate to the United States; it is *not only* because of the central role the United States has played on the development of economic globalization that favors First World countries at the expense of Third World countries from which the vast majority of us immigrants come. There is also the fact that, when it comes to deciding the central values that define and govern their existence, no people, society, nation, or government can ignore such a large part of its population as are the immigrants in the United States. To ignore the more than 28.4 million immigrants living in the United States, is to deprive us all of the immense contribution that such a large number of persons can and want to make to this country. Not to tap the richness of 10 percent of the population is a waste; it is being short-sighted, mindless, and outright unreasonable. It is simply impossible to comprehend or even fathom such attitudes unless one considers the fact that the United States has been a superpower in the world for nearly a century, and that those of the dominant group in this society continue to believe in Manifest Destiny, which today means that the American way of life is the best one there is and that the United States has the God-given task to bring it to every corner of the world.

Such waste is what affirmative action has been trying to correct for the last 50 years in the United States. Those of the dominant group in society think that affirmative action is a way of making up to those who were segregated from society and who are still being discriminated for what they have missed or endured. However, those of us who suffer ethnoracism, racism, and all sorts of prejudices that in a subtle but very efficient way continue to be present in this society, know very well that affirmative action is about having the possibility to contribute; it is about society recognizing the richness that diversity of experience, of life-circumstances, of background, and of culture can bring to this nation. It is precisely the richness of the diversity represented in such a high number of immigrants that can indeed prove to be a significant source of wisdom to capitalize on in the times of trouble for the United States. The economic system is broken; what are we to do? Do we patch up what we have and hope that the patch will hold? The political system is broken as the inability of Congress to function and the street protests of the system by the people during the whole of 2011 clearly show. What are we to do? Do we patch up the system and hope for the best? Or do we look at the root causes of the breakdown and dare to "dream dreams and see visions" (Joel 2:28 NRSV) in order to bring forth a government that is indeed "of the people, by the people, for the people"?

As an immigrant to the United States, I have always felt the obligation to contribute to the best of my ability to what we are as a people, as a society, as a nation, and to the government. There is great confusion regarding what these terms mean and unless we are clear, our contribution cannot be effective and/or can be easily ignored. Traditionally "people" has referred to a body of persons that are united by a common culture, tradition, or sense of kinship, and that typically have common language and beliefs. In our globalized world today, many countries—the word used in common parlance to refer to nation-states—are made up of more than one people; most countries, as a matter of fact, have to contend with more than one culture, with peoples of different traditions, who speak other than the language of the dominant group. Given this fact, people are held together more than anything else by beliefs, which here do not refer to religious beliefs but rather to values that the people cherish. In our globalized world, and in the frame of reference of a county, a people are those committed to be a society, to contribute to a society without losing the specificity of their own culture and the links to their countries of origin.

What is a society? "Society" adds to the elements of a people, an organizational framework, and refers to the patterns of relationships among the persons who constitute a people. It is in constructing a society that it is utterly unreasonable to ignore the richness that the diversity of the people can contribute. But for society to be for all the people, a government is needed. The government of a society guides society and manages the resources of the people so as to provide what each one needs to develop her or his human capabilities to the fullest; whether we do so or not is our individual choice. Finally, "nation" or "country" is the term used to refer to both society, which is constituted of peoples, and the government. Each of these entities, people, society, nation, and government, have their own specificity at the same time that they share attributes. In speaking of one, therefore, we are in a way also speaking of the other three.

The question before us today as a people, as a society and a nation, the question regarding our government, has to do with the values that must guide us. We go back to the values proclaimed at the founding of this nation, values that continue to be brandished by our society and our government: life, liberty, and the pursuit of happiness. In order to use them today, however, we have to understand how these values have been understood in ways that have caused repression and oppression for many: for the indigenous people, for the African Americans, for Latinas/os, for Asian Americans, for all those who do not belong to the dominant group, the Euro-Americans. In order to reimagine and refurbish who we are as a people and as a nation, we need to turn to all the peoples in this society and ask them what do they mean by life, liberty, and the pursuit of happiness, always remembering that in our globalized world, our self-understanding as a nation has to be such that it allows and supports the self-understanding of other nations. To give up the belief that the American way of life and the American system— the social, economic, and political way that we use in how we organize as a people, in how we operate as a society—is not the best one in the world and that we are not to impose it on others "for their own good," is a tall order. However, an even more difficult task is for this society to comprehend and accept that the American way of life and the American system is not good even for ourselves—for the majority of our peoples.

It is extremely difficult to begin to comprehend that there is a need for radical change in the American way of life and the American system, but great numbers of people in this country have begun to do so. The emergence of the Tea Party and their success in the 2010 elections was a call for radical change from the Right. By the Right I mean a social, economic, and political position that rejects—hardly ever openly, of course—social equality; embraces neoliberal economics that supports free markets, privatization of economic resources, and deregulation of the economy; and works to minimize the role of government when it comes to protection of all the peoples and providing what is needed for the good of all.

The call for radical change from the Left in 2011 has been persistent. A vast number of US citizens finally have realized that the "American Century," as the twentieth century has been called, has come to an end, a century that witnessed the United States attaining and enjoying the zenith of political and economic power. Early in 2011, the struggle in Milwaukee to protect the rights of workers to collective bargaining culminated in recall elections that unseated politicians who endorsed limiting such rights. Then came the Occupy Wall Street Movement in New York City that has now spread throughout the country and to many countries around the world with its uncompromising call for broad changes in social, economic, and governmental systems of the United States and other countries. Finally, consider the win in Ohio to suppress attempts similar to those in Wisconsin, and the recall in Arizona of one of the legislators responsible for the harsh anti-immigrant law in that state—yes, these are calls for radical change from the Left. By the Left here I mean a social, economic, and political position that focuses on the full development of everyone's human capabilities, for which cooperative and mutually respectful relations are needed. Such relations cannot thrive when excessive differences in status, power, and wealth exist. Furthermore, the Left believes that without substantial equality, not only the development of marginalized and oppressed people is made impossible, but that substantial inequality also undermines the rich-and-powerful's sense of being members of a society and of having social responsibility. The Left believes that the lack of resources the poor and oppressed have to develop their human capabilities, and the resentment and conflict engendered by sharp social and economic distinctions between the tiny number of rich people (1%) and the vast majority of the people (99%), are the main cause of the economic debacle in which the United States and the world at large finds itself today. Finally, when it comes to the government, the Left understands its role to be the protector of each and every one of its people. This means that government has a role to play, through regulations, in the fair distribution of basic goods in society; it has the responsibility to establish national programs that are for the good of all—that is, a national health-care system from which all can benefit, public schools and universities, a safety net for those who cannot provide for themselves, a program that can support the elderly, like Social Security; it has the obligation to maintain a safe environment for all in society; and in our globalized world, it has the responsibility to participate in creating and sustaining a world order that provides for all and respects the rights of all to social self-defining persons.

Latinas'/Latinos' Contribution to Redefining the United States

It is not difficult to see that being an ethnoracial group in the United States that suffers discrimination and has been welcomed only in so far as we renounce our culture and become assimilated by the culture of the dominant group, the majority of Latinas/os in the United States tend to endorse the ideas associated with the Left. Our contribution to redefining the American way of life and the American system is precisely in helping to redefine the meaning of life, liberty, and the pursuit of happiness, and to do so within the context of a globalized world, a world where colonization of any kind is not acceptable or possible. Our contribution is to help us as a society and help our government understand political integration in a way that does not destroy the richness of diversity and that there is a need for "establishing a broader 'we' based on . . . greater respect for, as well as appreciation, recognition, and preservation of, differences." (Mendieta 2003, 224) I do not claim that our understandings are unique, that no one else has them. On the contrary, I am aware that our understandings are shared by other peoples, which we take as a confirmation of the rectitude and goodness of our understandings. Our understandings are specifically ours, but not exclusively ours, not uniquely ours.

For Latinas/os life is a struggle—*la lucha*—that brings dignity and honor to ourselves and our families. Life, fullness of life, is not about having but about being, though we indeed know that unless we can satisfy our basic needs we cannot fully be and develop our human capabilities. Life for us happens in and thanks to our communities in which "we live and move and have our being" (Acts 17:28 NRSV), such as our families—extended families that consist not only of blood relatives but also of "political relatives" that we welcome for a variety of reasons; our local communities—our *barrios*—where we can be who we are, where our culture is respected and understood, where we are *hermanas, cuates, carnales, vatos, comadres, compañeros*—all of these terms stressing close relationship among people. The sense of *fiesta* is intrinsic to our concept of life: *fiesta*, which is usually translated as "party" but means much more to us. *Fiesta* is always a celebration of life. Circumstances might be difficult, very difficult, but that does not mean that we do not receive life as a gift and our *fiestas* are our grateful response to life. We might not have much, we might be ignored by the powerful and the rich, but that does not diminish who we are or how we see ourselves, because the meaning of life is not determined by the material goods we possess. For the vast majority of us, Latinas and Latinos, life is rooted in the divine. It is the divine among us—no matter how we understand or name the divine—that sustains our lives, gives meaning to our lives, and makes life possible no matter the circumstances in which we live.

Happiness for Latina and Latinos, as is true of everyone, is linked to our concept of life. The relational understanding of life that is central to Latino culture is the heart of our understanding of happiness. Though we do want material goods and work to have them and enjoy them—often falling into the grips of consumerism, which through advertisement turns wants into needs, and reduces happiness and life to having material possession for the sake of having them—happiness for us has less to do with material possessions than with the caring relationships we have and our passing on to the next generation our cultural values, rituals, and our struggles. There is a certain simplicity to happiness that is the result of living in poverty and as members of a community that suffers discrimination. Struggling mightily to make ends meet, to educate the children and take care of the elderly, while maintaining a sense of dignity and honor regardless of what the dominant group in society thinks about us, makes us appreciate the simple things of life. I have never been in more joyful celebrations than those of the grassroots Latinas and Latinos. The extravagance of the joy seems to make up for the simplicity of what we have to celebrate with: food made in our home kitchens, music either coming from a CD player or from some friend who plays the guitar while others of us play drums using a pot or even the wooden back of a chair and others rhythmically shake maracas or a *guiro*. Many of us not born in the United States never lose the hope that we will return to our lands of origin, or, if not, that we will at least be buried there. This includes many Puerto Ricans, for though their island is part of the United States, they continue to consider their island somewhat separate from the United States and long to be buried back home. For those of us who have been here for several generations, either because our ancestors came here in the hopes of a better future, or because the frontier crossed them—as it did at the end of the Mexican-American War to those living in what is now the southwest of the United States—happiness is about being with one's own with whom we can indeed feel at home, with whom we can be openly affectionate and not have to guard against wearing our emotions pinned to our sleeves. Relationality—a strong attachment to community and family—and a zest for life, this is what the pursuit of happiness is all about for us.

Liberty for Latinas and Latinos is also related to the importance of relationality for us. Individualism is not considered a virtue. We use the word *individuo*—individual—to refer to a person in a pejorative way. An *individuo* is one who is not rooted in the community, who does not care about others. Liberty is indeed about self-determination, about the ability to do for ourselves, to become the best person one can be. But self-determination is not attained individually but always in the midst of and through the relationships that sustain and make us who we are. Liberty for Latinas and Latinos is indeed about the ability to enjoy rights and privileges but not if they are at the expense of others. We are very careful to teach our children that to be free; to have liberty means that one is responsible for who one is and what one does. Liberty is not a matter of doing whatever one pleases; liberty is doing what one is able to do for one's own good and the good of family, friends, and communities.

Latinas and Latinos' concept of liberty, rooted in relationality and being a family and community matter and not an individual right, makes it very difficult for us to deal with the individualism that so marks the American way of life. Our children find it difficult to assert themselves individually, to see competitiveness as a driving force when cooperation, which marks relationships, is what they learn at home. Liberty has to do with being able to follow one's conscience without fear of punishment or diminishment. Therefore, liberty depends on educating our consciences in such a way that they guide us to be our best possible selves.

I am not in any way claiming that Latinas and Latinos are all virtuous, better than other peoples. All I am claiming is that the specific experiences we have, initially as Third World, and now Third World people living in the United States, experiences with "race and ethnicity, with exile and emigration, with bilingualism, with failed nationalism, with suspended or never granted citizenship, with religious acculturation, with the romance and disappointment of socialist revolutionary project," has afforded us "with vast historical memory." This may allow us, "to articulate new postnational, postglobal projects of humanization that speak in the name of a coming universalism in which many worlds are made possible." (Mendieta 2003, 229)

I am not claiming that Latina/o culture is better than any other of the cultures that have contributed and contribute to the American way of life. What I am trying to relate are the virtues that we uphold even as we fail to live them, the values that shape our culture and are the horizon of our lives, a horizon that we never reach but that is always before us. These cultural values are indeed the best gift we have to contribute to the US society, to the US nation. We claim our Latina/o culture and, as we continue to forge it in a very different situation from the historical realities in which it originated, we offer it as a resource "for the remaking of The United States into a new people." (Mendieta 2003, 228). It is our understanding of life, liberty, and the pursuit of happiness centered on relationality and care for others that we bring to this historical moment during which we seek to redefine the American way of life and the American system.

References

Bingham, John K. 2007. "To Leave or Not to Leave: the Right to Not Migrate and What the Church is Doing to Help People to Stay at Home." Building Bridges, Not Walls—Catholic Legal Immigration Network, Inc. National Conference May 2007, Tucson, AZ. Available at http://www.migrationanddevelopment.net/perspectives-positions/to-leave-or-not-to-leave-the-right-not-to-migrate-and-what-the-church-is-doing-to-help-people-stay-at-home. Accessed November 11, 2011.

Catholic Bishops of Mexico and the United States. 2003. *Strangers No Longer—Together on the Journey of Hope*. Available at http://www.vacatholic.org/documents/Immigrants-Strangers-No-Longer.pdf. Accessed November 11, 2011.

Catholic Relief Services. 2003. *Recommendations to the US Trade Representative during Negotiation of the Central American Free Trade Agreement*. Available at http://old.usccb.org/sdwp/international/crs.shtml. Accessed November 21, 2011.

Clark, Barry. 1998. *Political Economy: A Comparative Approach*. Westport, CT: Praeger Press.

Mendieta, Eduardo. 2003. "What Can Latinas/os Learn from Cornel West? The Latino Postcolonial Intellectual in the Age of the Exhaustion of Public Spheres." *Nepantla: Views from the South* 4.2: 213–233.

Stalker, Peter. 2000. *Workers Without Frontiers*. Geneva, Switzerland: International Labor Organization—ILO.

Straubhaar, Thomas. 2000. "Why Do We Need a General Agreement on Movements of People (GAMP)?" Discussion Paper, Hamburg Institute of International

Economics. Available at http://ageconsearch.umn.edu/bitstream/26332/1/dp000094.pdf. Accessed November 11, 2011.

Taran, Patrick A. 2000. "Human Rights of Migrants: Challenges of the New Decade." IOM/UN International Migration, Quarterly Review 38.6. Available at http://www.migrantwatch.org/Resources/challeges_new_decade.html. Accessed November 11, 2011.

United Nations Population Fund. 2006. "State of World Population—A Passage of Hope." Available at http://www.unfpa.org/swp/2006/english/chapter_1/index.html. Accessed November 11, 2011.

Wallach, Lori and Todd Tucker. 2006. "Debunking the Myth of Mode 4 and the U.S. H-1B Visa Program." Public Citizen's Global Trade Watch. Available at http://www.citizen.org/documents/Mode_Four_H1B_Visa_Memo.pdf. Accessed November 11, 2011.

Wilkinson, Jerry. "Influence of France on Florida." Historical Preservation Society of the Upper Keys. Available at http://www.keyshistory.org/FL-Fla-Fr.html. Accessed November 11, 2011.

Afterword

Mary McClintock Fulkerson and
Rosemary P. Carbine

Ada's closing essay is provocative for the future challenges set before public intellectuals. For example, take the deep ambiguity in the notion of "immigrants"; an honest telling of our nation's history dispels the prominent myth that distinguishes between "us" and "them" and beckons us toward a new myth on the horizon, and indeed is already alive here. Without romanticizing any marginalized group, Ada reminds us of the richness provided this country when the great variety of lives and forms of wisdom, which inform the essays in part I of this book, are taken seriously. How can this richness be honored? How can there be a concern for the common good of all, rather than a militarist and competitive capitalist power-driven logic that diminishes the well-being of many? Society and government are entailed in our "nation" and the main question, as Ada insists, is how to get these fundamental realities to support and promote values that honor all humans, rather than repeat updated versions of the oblivious and destructive practices that harmed indigenous peoples, African Americans, Latinas/os, Asian Americans and other so-called alien groups.

Based on the ways in which contributors to this volume are connected to a community of accountability that shapes their academic and activist work, academics will also continue to face the challenge to speak compellingly to publics about new—or redeemed—visions for and of this nation. That challenge includes the construction of new and creative ways to connect to other populations outside the academy. Given the increasing politics of fear and the anti-intellectual bias in

American culture, how can we better promote the notion that critical reflection has a key role to play in social and political transformation? How can we take seriously the role of intellectual work, make connections that matter, and avoid forms of academic tourism? How can we be critics and agents for change, yet avoid simplistic binaries of oppressor/oppressed? How can we recognize the harmful function of religious beliefs and practices in our nation, and also support the creative function of Christianity, of all religious beliefs and practices, for the social good, as pointed out particularly but not only in part II and III of this book? Given our own fallibility and our own socially located takes on reality, that is, given that at times public intellectuals undermine their own efforts to create change by failing to better address injustice within their own communities, we will inevitably fall short, even as we must continue to strive to make a better world.

Selected Bibliography of
Suggested Readings

Achbar, Mark and Peter Wintonick. *Manufacturing Consent: Noam Chomsky and the Media*. New York: Zeitgeist Films, 2002.

Alexander, Michelle. *The New Jim Crow: Mass Incarceration in the Age of Colorblindness*. Revised edition. New York: New Press, 2012.

Alfred, Gerald R. *Wasa'se: Indigenous Pathways of Action and Freedom*. Peterborough, Ont.and Orchard Park, NY: Broadview Press, 2005.

Althaus-Reid, Marcella. *Indecent Theology: Theological Perversions in Sex, Gender, and Politics*. London and New York: Routledge, 2000.

————. "Lunchtime Crucifixions: Theological Reflections on Economic Violence and Redemption." In *Weep Not for Your Children: Essays on Religion and Violence*, edited by Lisa Isherwood and Rosemary Radford Ruether. London: Equinox Publishing, 2008.

Anderson, Victor. *Pragmatic Theology: Negotiating the Intersections of an American Philosophy of Religion and Public Theology*. Albany: State University of New York Press, 1998.

Appiah, Kwame Anthony. *The Honor Code: How Moral Revolutions Happen*. New York: W. W. Norton, 2010.

Bageant, Joe. *Deer Hunting with Jesus: Dispatches from America's Class War*. New York: Crown Publishers, 2007.

Baker, Lee D. *Anthropology and the Racial Politics of Culture*. Durham, NC: Duke University Press, 2010.

Barker, D. and S. Feiner. *Liberating Economics*. Ann Arbor: University of Michigan Press, 2005.

Benhabib, Seyla. *The Claims of Culture: Equality and Diversity in the Global Era*. Princeton, NJ and Oxford: Princeton University Press, 2002.

Benhabib, Seyla, ed. *Democracy and Difference: Contesting the Boundaries of the Political*. Princeton, NJ: Princeton University Press, 1996.

Boone, Sylvia Ardyn. *Radiance from the Waters: Ideals of Feminine Beauty in Mende Art*. New Haven, CT: Yale University Press, 1986.

Brock, Rita Nakashima. "Occupy Oakland: Reflections from the Alameda County Jail." Available at http://www.huffingtonpost.com/rita-nakashima-brock-ph-d

/occupy-oakland-reflections-alameda-county-jail_b_1097834.html. Accessed November 21, 2011.

————. "Why Occupy Oakland Persists in Searching for a Home." Available at http://www.huffingtonpost.com/rita-nakashima-brock-ph-d/why-occupy-oakland-persists_b_1240784.html. Accessed on January 30, 2012.

Brock, Rita Nakashima and Rebecca Ann Parker. *Saving Paradise: How Christianity Traded Love of This World for Crucifixion and Empire*. Boston: Beacon Press, 2008.

Brooten, Bernadette J., ed. *Beyond Slavery: Overcoming its Religious and Sexual Legacies*. New York: Palgrave Macmillan, 2010.

Butler, Judith. *Frames of War: When is Life Grievable?* London and New York: Verso, 2009.

Butler, Judith and Joan W. Scott, eds. *Feminists Theorize the Political*. New York and London: Routledge, 1992.

Casanova, José. *Public Religions in the Modern World*. Chicago and London: University of Chicago Press, 1994.

Cavanaugh, William T., Jeffrey W. Bailey, and Craig Hovey, eds. *An Eerdmans Reader in Contemporary Political Theology*. Grand Rapids, MI: Eerdmans, 2012.

Chow, Rey. *The Age of the World Target: Self-Referentiality in War, Theory and Comparative Work*. Durham, NC: Duke University Press, 2006.

Cobb, John B. *Is It Too Late?: A Theology of Ecology*. Denton, TX: Environmental Ethics Books, 1995.

Cone, James H. *Martin and Malcolm and America: A Dream or a Nightmare*. Maryknoll, NY: Orbis Books, 1992.

Conrad, C., J. Whitehead, P. Mason, and J. Stewart, eds. *African Americans and the U.S. Economy*. Lanham, MD: Rowman and Littlefield, 2005.

Copeland, M. Shawn. *Enfleshing Freedom: Body, Race, and Being*. Minneapolis: Fortress Press, 2009.

Crouter, Richard. *Reinhold Niebuhr: On Politics, Religion, and Christian Faith*. New York and Oxford: Oxford University Press, 2010.

Daly, Mary. *Beyond God the Father: Toward a Philosophy of Women's Liberation*. Boston: Beacon, 1993, 1973.

Danticat, Edwige. *Create Dangerously: The Immigrant Artist at Work*. Princeton, NJ: Princeton University Press, 2010.

Davis, Angela Y. *Women, Race, & Class*. New York: Vintage Books, 1983.

Doak, Mary. *Reclaiming Narrative for Public Theology*. Albany: State University of New York Press, 2004.

Douglass, Frederick. Independence Day speech, Rochester. July 5, 1852. Available at http://teachingamericanhistory.org/library/index.asp?document=162. Accessed May 28, 2012.

Engels, Friedrich. *The Origin of the Family: Private Property and the State*. Honolulu: University Press of the Pacific, 2001, 1902.

Espinosa, Gaston, ed. *Religion, Race, and the American Presidency*. Lanham, MD : Rowman and Littlefield, 2011.

Fanon, Frantz. *The Wretched of the Earth*. New York: Grove Press, 2004, 1963.

Fernandez, Eleazar S. and Fernando F. Segovia, eds. *A Dream Unfinished: Theological Reflections on America from the Margins*. Maryknoll, NY: Orbis Books, 2001.

Floyd Thomas, Stacey, ed. *Deeper Shades of Purple: Womanism in Religion and Society*. New York: New York University Press, 2006.

Gilroy, Paul. *Against Race: Imagining Political Culture Beyond the Color Line*. Cambridge, MA: Belknap Press, 2002.

————. *"There Ain't No Black in the Union Jack": The Cultural Politics of Race and Nation*. Chicago: University of Chicago Press, 1991.

Goldman, Emma. *Anarchism and Other Essays*. 3rd revised edition. New York: Mother Earth Publishing Association; London: A. C. Fifield, 1917.

Gottlieb, Roger S. *Joining Hands: Politics and Religion Together for Social Change*. Cambridge, MA: Westview Press, 2002.

Greider, William. "The Democratic Promise of Occupy Wall Street." Available at http://www.thenation.com/article/164767/democratic-promise-occupy-wall-street. Accessed on November 22, 2011.

Gutiérrez, Gustavo. *A Theology of Liberation: History, Politics, and Salvation*. Maryknoll, NY: Orbis Books, 1988, c1973.

Hardt, Michael. *Commonwealth*. Cambridge, MA: Belknap Press of Harvard University Press, 2009.

Harvey, David. *Cosmopolitanism and the Geographies of Freedom*. New York: Columbia University Press, 2009.

Henderson, Sarah L. and Alana S. Jeydel. *Participation and Protest: Women and Politics in a Global World*. New York and Oxford: Oxford University Press, 2007.

Heyer, Kristin E., Mark J. Rozell, and Michael A. Genovese, eds. *Catholics and Politics: The Dynamic Tension between Faith and Power*. Washington, DC: Georgetown University Press, 2008.

Himes, Michael J. and Kenneth R. Himes. *Fullness of Faith: The Public Significance of Theology*. New York and Mahwah, NJ: Paulist Press, 1993.

Hollenbach, David. *The Global Face of Public Faith: Politics, Human Rights, and Christian Ethics*. Washington, DC: Georgetown University Press, 2003.

hooks, bell. *Outlaw Culture: Resisting Representations*. New York: Routledge, 2006, 1994.

————. *Yearning: Race, Gender, and Cultural Politics*. Boston: South End Press, 1999.

Hopkins, Dwight N., ed. *Black Faith and Public Talk: Critical Essays on James H. Cone's Black Theology and Black Power*. Maryknoll, NY: Orbis, 1999.

Hurston, Zora Neale. *The Sanctified Church*. Berkeley, CA: Turtle Island Press, 1981.

Iwamura, Jane Naomi. *Virtual Orientalism: Asian Religions and American Popular Culture*. New York: Oxford University Press, 2011.

Johnson, Walter. *Soul by Soul: Life inside the Antebellum Slave Market*. Cambridge, MA: Harvard University Press 1999.

Jones, Robert P. *Progressive and Religious: How Christian, Jewish, Muslim, and Buddhist Leaders are Moving Beyond the Culture Wars and Transforming American Life.* Lanham, MD: Rowman and Littlefield, 2008.

Kelley, Robin D. G. *Freedom Dreams: The Black Radical Imagination.* Boston: Beacon Press, 2002.

———. *Yo' Mama's Disfunktional!: Fighting the Culture Wars in Urban America.* Boston: Beacon Press, 1997.

Khanna, Ranjana. *Algeria Cuts: Women and Representation, 1830 to the Present.* Stanford, CA: Stanford University Press, 2008.

Kim, Jodi. *Ends of Empire: Asian American Critique and the Cold War.* Minneapolis: University of Minnesota Press, 2010.

Kwok, Pui-lan. *Postcolonial Imagination and Feminist Theology.* Louisville, KY: Westminster John Knox Press, 2005.

Landes, Joan B., ed. *Feminism, the Public and the Private.* New York: Oxford University Press, 1998.

Lewis, Kristen and Sarah Burd-Sharps, eds. *The Measure of America, 2010–201.* New York: New York University Press 2010.

Lorde, Audre. *Sister Outsider: Essays and Speeches.* Trumansburg, NY: Crossing Press, 1984.

Lovin, Robin, ed. *Religion and American Public Life: Interpretations and Explorations.* New York: Paulist, 1986.

Marable, Manning. *How Capitalism Underdeveloped Black America: Problems in Race, Political Economy, and Society.* Updated edition. Cambridge, MA: South End Press, 2000.

Marable, Manning and Kristen Clarke, eds. *Barack Obama and African American Empowerment: The Rise of Black America's New Leadership.* New York: Palgrave Macmillan, 2009.

Martinez, Gaspar. *Confronting the Mystery of God: Political, Liberation, and Public Theologies.* New York: Continuum, 2001.

Marty, Martin E. *The Public Church: Mainline—Evangelical—Catholic.* New York: Crossroad, 1981.

Marty, Martin E. and Jonathan Moore. *Politics, Religion, and the Common Good: Advancing a Distinctly American Conversation about Religion's Role in Our Shared Life.* San Francisco: Jossey-Bass, 2000.

Matsuoka, Fumitaka and Eleazar S. Fernandez, eds. *Realizing the America of Our Hearts: Theological Voices of Asian Americans.* St. Louis, MO: Chalice Press, 2003.

Mendieta, Eduardo and Jonathan VanAntwerpen, eds. *The Power of Religion in the Public Sphere.* New York: Columbia University Press, 2011.

Mitchem. Stephanie Y. *African American Folk Healing.* New York: New York University Press, 2007.

———. *African American Women Tapping Power and Spiritual Wellness.* Cleveland, OH: Pilgrim Press, 2004; Wipf and Stock reprint 2010.

Moraga, Cherrie L. and Gloria E. Anzaldua, eds. *This Bridge Called My Back: Writings by Radical Women of Color.* 3rd edition. Berkeley, CA: Third Woman Press, 2002.

Negri, Antonio. *The Savage Anomaly: The Power of Spinoza's Metaphysics and Politics*. Minneapolis: University of Minnesota Press, 1991.

Nicholls, David G. *Conjuring the Folk: Forms of Modernity in African America*. Ann Arbor: University of Michigan Press, 2000.

Niebuhr, H. Richard. *Christ and Culture*. New York: HarperCollins, 2001 [1951].

O'Brien, David J. *Public Catholicism*. 2nd edition. Maryknoll, NY: Orbis Books, 1996.

Okihiro, Gary. *Margins and Mainstreams: Asians in American History and Culture*. Seattle: University of Washington Press, 1994.

———. *Common Ground: Reimagining American History*. Princeton, NJ: Princeton University Press, 2001.

Omi, Michael and Howard Winant. *Racial Formation in the United States from the 1960s to the 1990s*. New York: Routledge, 1994.

Payne, Ruby K. *A Framework for Understanding Poverty*. 4th revised edition. Highlands, TX: aha! Process, 1996, 2005.

Pinker, Steven. *The Better Angels of Our Nature: Why Violence Has Declined*. New York: Viking, 2011.

Prashad, Vijay. *The Darker Nations: A People's History of the Third World*. New York and London: New Press, 2008.

Recinos, Harold J., ed. *Wading Through Many Voices: Toward a Theology of Public Conversation*. Lanham, MD: Rowman and Littlefield, 2011.

Ricoeur, Paul. *The Symbolism of Evil*. Boston: Beacon Press, 1969, 1967.

Ruether, Rosemary Radford. *Gaia and God: An Ecofeminist Theology of Earth Healing*. New York: Harper Collins, 1992.

Said, Edward W. *Orientalism*. New York: Vintage Books, 2003, 1978.

Scott, Peter and William T. Cavanaugh, eds. *The Blackwell Companion to Political Theology*. Malden, MA: Blackwell, 2003.

Seager, Joni. *Penguin Atlas of Women in the World*. 4th edition. New York: Penguin Books 2009.

Staples, Robert. "The Myth of Black Macho: A Response to Angry Black Feminists." *Black Scholar* 10 (March/April 1979), 25.

Sturm, Douglas. *Solidarity and Suffering: Toward a Politics of Relationality*. Albany: State University of New York Press, 1998.

Takaki, Ronald T. *Iron Cages: Race and Culture in 19th Century America*. Revised edition. New York: Oxford University Press, 2000.

Thiemann, Ronald F. *Constructing a Public Theology: The Church in a Pluralistic Culture*. Louisville, KY: Westminster John Knox Press, 1991.

———. *Religion in Public Life: A Dilemma for Democracy*. Washington, DC: Georgetown University Press, 1996.

Tinker, George E. *Spirit and Resistance: Political Theology and American Indian Liberation*. Minneapolis, MN: Fortress Press, 2004.

Townes, Emilie M. *Womanist Ethics and the Cultural Production of Evil*. New York: Palgrave Macmillan, 2006.

Valentin, Benjamin. *Mapping Public Theology: Beyond Culture, Identity, and Difference*. Harrisburg, PA: Trinity Press International, 2002.

Wallace, Michele. *Black Macho and the Myth of the Superwoman.* New York: Warner Books, 1980.

West, Cornel. *Democracy Matters: Winning the Fight Against Imperialism.* New York: Penguin Press, 2004.

———. *Race Matters.* New York: Vintage Books, 2001.

Willis, Deborah, ed. *Black Venus 2010.* Philadelphia: Temple University Press, 2010.

Wilson, Angela Cavender. *What Does Justice Look Like?: The Struggle for Liberation in Dakota Homeland.* St. Paul, MN: Living Justice Press, 2008.

Wolff, Richard D. *Capitalism Hits the Fan: The Global Economic Meltdown and What To Do About It.* Northampton, MA: Olive Branch Press, 2010.

Wuthnow, Robert. *Saving America?: Faith-Based Services and the Future of Civil Society.* Princeton, NJ: Princeton University Press, 2004.

Young, Iris Marion. *Inclusion and Democracy.* New York and Oxford: Oxford University Press, 2000.

———. *Justice and the Politics of Difference.* Princeton, NJ: Princeton University Press, 1990.

Zinn, Howard. *The Zinn Reader: Writings on Disobedience and Democracy.* 2nd edition, updated and expanded. New York: Seven Stories Press, 2009.

Zweig, Michael. *The Working Class Majority: America's Best Kept Secret.* 2nd edition. Ithaca, NY and London: ILR Press, 2012.

Contributors

Rosemary P. Carbine (MA and PhD, University of Chicago Divinity School) is visiting assistant professor of Religious Studies and director of fellowships at Whittier College. Carbine specializes in historical and contemporary Christian theologies, with a particular focus on theological anthropology, public/political theology, comparative feminist, womanist, and *mujerista* theologies, and teaching theology and religion. She has published widely on these topics in major reference works, scholarly journals, and books, including *Monika Hellwig: The People's Theologian* (2010), *Frontiers in Catholic Feminist Theology* (2009), *Prophetic Witness: Catholic Women's Strategies of Reform* (2009), and *Cross-Examinations: Readings on the Meaning of the Cross Today* (2006). She is currently contributing coeditor for *Women, Wisdom, and Witness: Engaging Contexts in Conversation* (2012). Bridging activism in US Catholic feminist movements with these academic interests, Carbine has served as cochair of the Feminist Theory and Religious Reflection Group within the American Academy of Religion, and presently coconvenes the Women's Consultation on Constructive Theology in the Catholic Theological Society of America. Considering the classroom a site of public engagement to shape undergraduate students for informed and responsible citizenship, she regularly offers courses on women and liberation theologies, comparative religious asceticism and activism, religion and US public life, and Christianity and US social justice movements, which utilize transformative pedagogies (such as theatre for social change and service/community-based learning) to help students find and rehearse their own critical theo-political voices, visions, and praxis.

Paula M. Cooey serves as the Margaret Weyerhaeuser Harmon Professor of Religion at Macalester College. A graduate of Harvard University (PhD), Harvard Divinity School (MTS), and the University of Georgia (BA), she teaches courses in the history of Christian traditions,

Christianity and culture, ethics, and theory of religion. She has written several books and articles; most of her published scholarship focuses on gender, environmental, and race-class issues in religious contexts, and her most recently published work has advocated for children. Cooey's latest book *Willing the Good: Jesus, Dissent, & Desire*, published by Augsburg Fortress Press, was released in summer 2006. Appointed to the Macalester faculty in 1999, she currently focuses her research on what it means to understand religion by examining religious life and practice in contexts of conflict, disruption, and assimilation, compared with other religious traditions and with secularism; her major project on this subject is tentatively titled "Getting Religion." Cooey self-describes as an aging white feminist teacher-scholar-activist who has tried to integrate her religious, political, and economic concerns with her academic training. An elder in the Presbyterian Church (USA), Cooey has taught and published for more than 30 years in different regions of the country—New England, the south/southwest, and the upper middle west. Her activism in the past has varied from work in the Civil Rights movement and in the first battered women's shelter in the country, to protest against nuclear armament and the various wars in which the United States has engaged over the last 50 years.

Teresa Delgado is associate professor of Religious Studies at Iona College, where she also serves as the director of Peace and Justice Studies. The intersection of theology and ethics—what we believe and how we act upon that belief—is where Delgado situates herself as a public intellectual. To fulfill her conviction that she must not only speak a prophetic word informed by the Gospel but also act upon that word in the world, she is involved in her local community, particularly as a board member of the Westchester Peace Action Coalition. In this work, Delgado is committed to embody a justice-centered faith alongside others whose own traditions lead them to seek justice and love in the world.

James H. Evans Jr. is the Robert K. Davies Professor of Systematic Theology at Colgate Rochester Crozer Divinity School. He is the author of *We Have Been Believers: An African American Systematic Theology* (2012; 1993); *Playing: Christian Explorations of Daily Living* (2010); *We Shall All Be Changed: Social Problems and Theological Renewal* (1997); *Black Theology: A Critical Assessment and Annotated Bibliography* (1987); and *Spiritual Empowerment in Afro-American Literature* (1988). Evans appraises social location as one of the most critical aspects of academic work. Intellectual inquiry requires not only that the writer identify the problems and possibilities inherent in his or her subject-matter but also that the writer clearly identify his or her own point of departure. Undergraduate studies in political science and English literature at the University of Michigan introduced Evans to the joys and problems of textual interpretation, and to the distribution of power in ways that enhance community or are directed only toward personal gain and private aggrandizement. While in college, Evans received a call to ministry and while in seminary at Yale Divinity School and then Union Theological Seminary, he discovered a love for theology. Over the course of his career, he has woven together these varied trajectories in an attempt to understand the world in which we live and the role that faith plays in it.

Ordained in the Presbyterian Church (USA), **Mary McClintock Fulkerson** is professor of Theology at Duke University Divinity School. Convinced that theology must connect to the practices of lived faith, she examined the liberating practices of feminist academics and non-feminist church women in her book *Changing the Subject: Women's Discourses and Feminist Theology.* Her ethnographic study of an interracial church that included people with disabilities, led to *Places of Redemption: Theology for a Worldly Church,* a book on ecclesial practices that resist racism and able-ism. She coedited *The Oxford Handbook of Feminist Theology,* essays on feminist theology and globalization, with Sheila Briggs. In the early 1990s, Fulkerson was part of a group that eventuated in the creation of Durham-CAN, a local organization that is a member of the Industrial Areas Foundation (IAF), a national grassroots network for social change. She has just joined Scholars for a Progressive North Carolina, and is also part of the Pauli Murray Project: Activating History for Social Change, a Duke Human Rights Center project generating conversations in the community about white privilege and the racial dynamics in Durham, North Carolina. The project uses the story of activist lawyer Pauli Murray, the first African American woman Episcopal priest, to get people to recover their own family histories in relation to marginalizing factors that shaped Murray's life, that is, race, gender, and sexual orientation.

A mentor, inspiration, and godmother for us all, **Ada María Isasi-Díaz** was born and raised in La Habana, Cuba. Based on her own experience as a political refugee and her lifelong dialogue with other women-centered theologies and liberation theologies around the globe, she became a tireless activist for the marginalized, not simply acknowledging their needs, but mainly providing a platform for their voices. The inventor of *mujerista* theology, which recognized the agency and creativity of

Hispanic women, Ada wrote many groundbreaking books. Among them are *Hispanic Women—Prophetic Voice in the Church: Toward a Hispanic Women's Liberation Theology* (1988), *Women of God, Women of the People* (1995), *Mujerista Theology: A Theology for the 21st Century* (1996), *En la lucha = In the Struggle: Elaborating a Mujerista Theology* (2004), and *La Lucha Continues: Mujerista Theology* (2004). Following her experience of solidarity with the poor as a missionary in the Order of St. Ursula in Lima, Peru, she became part of the feminist movement, inspired by the first Women's Ordination Conference. After earning both a master's of divinity degree and doctoral degree in Christian ethics at Union Theological Seminary, Ada served as professor of Ethics and Theology in the Theological School and Graduate Division of Religion at Drew University from 1991 to 2009. Between 1997 and 2004, Isasi-Díaz visited Cuba annually to participate in workshops, give lectures, and teach at the Protestant seminary in Matanzas. When Isasi-Díaz died in May 2012, she was at work on a book titled *Justicia: A Reconciliatiory Praxis of Care and Tenderness* regarding the central role of reconciliation to justice, to discovering, together with those from whom we have been apart, how to build a common future. Her employment of such themes as *lo cotidiano* (the everyday), *la lucha* (the struggle), and *fuerzas para la lucha* (God-given strength for the struggle) shape this book and continue to impact the wider world of religious public intellectuals.

Stephanie Y. Mitchem is professor and Chair of Religious Studies at the University of South Carolina, where she lives out a commitment to liberatory educational practice. She teaches contemporary theology and women's studies, emphasizing the experiences and perspectives of Black women, both in the United States and in the African Diaspora. Her research focuses on the intersections of social class, gender constructions, racism, and religions. Mitchem is a contributing editor of *Crosscurrents*, author of *African American Women Tapping Power and Spiritual Wellness* (2004), *Introducing Womanist Theology* (2002), and numerous essays. Her most recent books include: *Faith, Health, and Healing Among African Americans*, coedited with Emilie M. Townes (2008), *African American Folk Healing* (2007), and *Name It and Claim It? Prosperity Preaching and the Black Church* (2007). Mitchem self-describes as an African American woman from the working class, and thus her scholarship on African American women's religious lives begins by asking questions based on the cognitive dissonances between lived life and theories posed across many disciplines that do not speak of the realities of Black lives, women's experiences, and oppressed situations; this is especially true of those scholars who try to use white American / European life as some standardized measurement. Integrated into Mitchem's research and work on African American and women's religious lives are companion issues of human rights, education, and politics. Therefore, Mitchem uses tools of intellectual history, social theory, and ethnography/anthropology to analyze nation, race, class, ethnicity, and gender. Writing about and teaching from these parameters are critical forms of activism, especially in this time of bumper sticker philosophies.

Keun-Joo Christine Pae is assistant professor of Religion at Denison University's Department of Religion (Granville, OH). As a transitional diaconate, she is currently serving Trinity Episcopal Church in Newark, Ohio and expecting to be ordained a priest at her home diocese of Newark, New Jersey in December 2012. Through adult and youth education programs, Pae has been sharing her commitment to social justice and spiritual activism with ordinary Christians. During doctoral work at Union Theological Seminary in the City of New York, she volunteered at Rainbow Center, the first nonprofit organization for ex-Korean military wives. Since then, her research has focused on faith-based organizations' global peacemaking, the militarized sex industry, and the US military foreign policy. Her work is seeking effective communication between society and academia for global justice and peace. Taking the classroom as a site for social transformation, Pae has encouraged her students to critically engage social media, and religious teachings, and to interview social activists. She regularly writes an essay for *Ecumenian*, a Korean website for progressive Christians. Her essays include women and peacemaking, the US-Korea Free Trade Agreement, and Palestinian and Israeli conflict from a woman's perspective. Recent publications include: "A Solidarity-Talk among Women of Color: Creating the 'We' Category as a Liberative Feminist Method" in *Faith, Feminism, and Scholarship: Next Generation*, edited by Melanie Harris and Kate Ott (2011).

Anthony B. Pinn is the Agnes Cullen Arnold Professor of Humanities and Professor of Religious Studies at Rice University, where he also serves as the director of Graduate Studies. His studies of the nature and meaning of Black religion culminated in *Terror and Triumph: The Nature of Black Religion* (2003). In addition, Pinn is also the author/editor of 15 other books, including *Varieties of African American Religious Experience*; *The Black Church in the Post-Civil Rights Era*; *Why, Lord?: Suffering and Evil in Black Theology*; and *African American Humanist Principles: Living and Thinking Like the Children of Nimrod*. Pinn self-describes as a middle-class African American male, committed to the ability of lived ideas to transform thought and life. Much of Pinn's activism revolves around the promotion of humanistic ethics and praxis as a means by which to better live out democratic principles within the public arena. This involves work with African Americans for Humanism, the American Humanist Association, the Humanist Institute, the Unitarian Universalist Association, and the Institute for Humanist Studies.

Joerg Rieger is the Wendland-Cook Endowed Professor of Constructive Theology at the Perkins School of Theology at Southern Methodist University. Recent publications include *Traveling: Christian Explorations of Daily Living* (2011), *Globalization and Theology* (2010), *No Rising Tide: Theology, Economics, and the Future* (2009), and *Christ and Empire: From Paul to Postcolonial Times* (2007). For many years, Rieger has been actively involved in issues of religion and labor. He is co-convenor of a Workers' Rights Board in the North Texas area, through Jobs with Justice, which supports mainly those workers who do not have the opportunity to unionize, particularly immigrant workers. In the past, he has been involved in community organizing, in protection of the environment, and he continues to be involved in matters of women's liberation. Convinced that all forms of oppression are inter-related, Rieger argues for the deep solidarity of the liberation struggles that mark our age.

Andrea Smith is associate professor in the Department of Media and Cultural Studies at University of California, Riverside. Smith received her PhD in History of Consciousness at University of California, Santa Cruz in 2002. Previously, she taught in the Program in American Culture at the University of Michigan. Her publications include: *Native Americans and the Christian Right: The Gendered Politics of Unlikely Alliances* and *Conquest: Sexual Violence and American Indian Genocide*. She is also the editor *of The Revolution Will Not Be Funded: Beyond the Nonprofit Industrial Complex*, and coeditor of *The Color of Violence, The Incite! Anthology*. She currently serves as the US Coordinator for the Ecumenical Association of Third World Theologians, and she is a cofounder of both Incite! Women of Color Against Violence and the Boarding School Healing Project. Smith has been involved in the anti-violence movement and indigenous rights struggles for over 20 years; she recently completed a report for the United Nations on Indigenous Peoples and Boarding Schools.

Mark Lewis Taylor is Maxwell M. Upson Professor of Theology and Culture at Princeton Theological Seminary. His newly completed book is *The Theological and the Political: On the Weight of the World* (2011). Taylor received the Best General Interest Book Award of 2001 for *The Executed God: The Way of the Cross in Lockdown America* (2000), which proposed a Christian theology resistant to US empire in light of the prison-industrial complex, police brutality, and the death penalty. He is also founder of Educators for Mumia Abu-Jamal, a group of teachers from all levels of education, organizing since 1995 for a new trial on behalf of Abu-Jamal, a journalist who was on Pennsylvania's death row for 30 years, until 2011, when activists got him moved off death row to general population. Taylor has also been an activist in other movements to end US war (cofounder of the Coalition for Justice in Iraq, Princeton, NJ), for abolition of the death penalty, for immigration rights and reform, and for change in US policy toward Mexico and Latin America. Among his other books are *Religion, Politics and the Christian Right: Post-9/11 Politics and American Empire* (2005), and *Remembering Esperanza: A Cultural-Political Theology for North American Praxis* (2005 edition). Taylor now lives in Evanston, Illinois, since 2009, and commutes to Princeton where he remains a full-time professor.

Sharon Welch is professor of Religion and Society and the provost at Meadville Lombard Theological School. Welch is a social ethicist and public intellectual. Welch is the author of five books: *Real Peace, Real Security: The Challenges of Global Citizenship*; *After Empire: The Art and Ethos of Enduring Peace*; *A Feminist Ethic of Risk*; *Sweet Dreams in America: Making Ethics and Spirituality Work*; and *Communities of Resistance and Solidarity*. In her research and activism, she has worked primarily on four issues: strategic peacebuilding, racial justice, democratic dialogue, and moving from political critique to institutional transformation. Welch is a member of the International Steering Committee of Global Action to Prevent War, and a member of the Unitarian Universalist Peace Ministry Network; she has written widely on the practical measures that can build peace and prevent war. She has worked for racial justice through the development of curricula for teachers and seminarians and through shaping institutional policies and procedures. She has worked with undergraduates and seminarians to develop the skills of democratic deliberation, and with social change agents to amplify their power to shape sustainable, just institutions.

Index